TRAIN
A PARENT

By Scot and Holly Anderson

Train Up a Parent
Copyright © 2022 by Scot and Holly Anderson

All rights reserved. No part of this book may be reproduced or transmitted in any form or by any means without written permission from the author.

Printed in USA

To our five incredible children Laken, Heath, Baylor, Peyton, and Savannah. Without you, we would have never become parents.

IMPORTANT

This book is meant to be a companion to the teaching videos.

When you read something, you retain about 15-25%. If you read something and watch a video, you retain over 50%. If you read something, watch a video, and then discuss it, you retain over 80%. Based on this we have developed a class like system for parents. Each chapter accompanies a 30-minute teaching by Holly and me.

This book is meant to be shared with a group of other parents, parents to be, and grandparents in a group of 5-10 people. You meet weekly, go over the homework, and discuss for about 30 minutes. Then, you watch the next week's video together. Make it a time of fellowship—host a potluck, or snacks and drinks.

The group is what people like the most about this program. You'll find that you are not alone in the problems you face, and that getting other people's perspective and ideas are priceless. They say it takes a village to raise a child. This program, in a sense, is your village. Many people find lifelong friends in this setting. Don't let feelings like "we aren't good enough parents, or we don't know the material" dissuade you from being a leader. Leading helps you learn more than you would just going through it. It is also a strength to say, we don't have it figured out.

This book has videos for each chapter:

https://www.youtube.com/playlist?list=PLoQ8_Hx6LYyjU9Io5HVIpXLtqG9OBY70G.

The easiest way to find the videos is to search out Living Word Bible Church on YouTube, then go into playlist. You will see the "Train Up a Parent" playlist. You can also search out Wake Up daily Bible study. This is a daily Bible study, provided by my me and my brother. It is the number one Bible study on YouTube. Or search for Scot Anderson, and from there, you can click on living word and find the playlist. All the videos are absolutely free.

We challenge you to go through this series every year. You will always hear and retain the information for the season of parenting you are in. Parents also tend to slide back into bad habits and forget key steps to raising kids. Holly and I taught this class every year for decades. Every time we taught it, we would finish with a chapter and say to ourselves, "we've got to get back to doing that."

If you ever have questions, please find me on Facebook. I am one of the few mega-pastors who answer my direct messages on Facebook. We are excited to see what great parenting produces in your life. You can also go to our train up a parent page on Facebook.

Scot and Holly

CHAPTER 1:
Imagine a World Where Kids Did What You Asked

The Day from Hell (Actually, Every Day)

Your day starts as you try to get up early enough to prepare, makeup on, dressed for the battle ahead. Another horrible night's sleep! Your two-year-old was up all night long. She still sleeps in your bed, of course. Just as you turn on the bath, you hear the screaming of your suddenly awake Johnny, four years old. His screams wake Ashley, your two-year-old. It is six o'clock. The kids want their breakfast, and they want it now. Why wouldn't they? You get their breakfast every morning, just as soon as they start screaming.

You rush downstairs, Ashley in hand, because you fear that you will emotionally scar them if they wait too long to eat. You try to change Ashley's diaper while Johnny is screaming and pulling on your robe.

"I'M HUNGRYYYY, IM HUNGRY, I'M HUNGRY!!"

These words bore into your throbbing head. "I know, Sweetie. Give mommy a minute to change Ashley."

"NO, I WANT IT NOW!!!"

You take the crew into the kitchen, set Ashley in her chair, give her a granola bar, and then turn to Johnny. "Here, Sweetie. Mommy will make you some toast for breakfast."

"I DON'T WANT TOAST!" the child exclaims.

"Okay, how about some eggs and bacon?"

"NO!"

"Okay, what about Cheerios?"

"NO!"

"What about a bagel?" A sinking feeling says that you are running out of options.

"NO, I want *Cap'n Crunch*."

"We ran out of that yesterday."

Johnny is in full voice, now. "WAH!!!!! Wah!!!!"

You must immediately comfort the child, right? You're scared that the scarring of his soul has already taken place.

"Mommy will get more cereal today at the store. I promise!" After minutes with pleading to the child, Johnny finally stops crying. Meanwhile, he's agreed to settle for *Sugar Puffs*.

As you begin to pour the cereal in the bowl, the child screams, "I DON'T WANT THE BLUE BOWL, I WANT THE GREEN ONE!"

"Okay, Sweetie," you say as you pour the cereal out of the bowl and back into the box, then go get the green bowl. You might have just poured the cereal from one bowl to another, but you're frazzled.

Just then, you look over and find that Ashley has granola bar everywhere—in her hair, diaper, and all over the floor. "Ashley! you know better!" You pick her up and take her to the sink to clean up.

Johnny begins to cry. "I WANT MY CEREAL!!!"

"I know, Sweetie. Mom is going to get it for you." While he continues to cry, you clean Ashley up and put her back in her seat, along with a bowl (what color did you choose?) of dry *Sugar Puffs*. For reasons unknown to you and maybe even to God, she begins to cry too.

You don't have time for that. You have Johnny to attend to. You grab the green bowl, pour the cereal, and race over to Johnny. Finally, you pour him a glass of milk.

He screams again. "I DON'T WANT MILK. I WANT JUICE!"

You pour out the milk (no time to put it back in the bottle!) and get him a glass of juice.

He screams, "I don't want that cup. I want my *Power Ranger* cup!"

How could you have been so stupid? You grab his favorite cup and fill it with juice. A glance at Ashley reminds you—she's crying, too. What is she angry about? Guessing, you decide that she wants a bowl like brother. Fine. You go get it and—wonder of wonders—everybody is eating and happy.

Breakfast is done. Now you ask Johnny what he wants to do. He says, "I want to play with my train."

"Honey, why don't we play with the new Lego's we got you? Maybe the matchbox cars?"

"I WANT THE TRAIN!"

"But Honey, the train is put away and it is a lot of work to get it out." Before you even finish, a new fit begins. You capitulate in moments. "Okay, let's get the train."

You get the train down, out of the box, and after some painstaking setup, you say, "Here, play while Mom goes and gets ready." The long day stretches ahead, and you need to get ready.

Before you reach the steps, you hear a battle cry from the room behind you. You rush in to see Johnny and Ashley holding onto the same train, screaming and tugging at it. This is not your first time as a referee. After ten minutes of coaxing each child, you finally bring peace to the tribe.

The bathroom awaits, but halfway up the stairs, the battle starts anew. You realize that it will be impossible for you to go upstairs. You have to stay and keep the peace. You spend the next hour subduing the tantrums and just barely holding onto your sanity.

An eternity later, it's time for lunch. You say, "Time to clean up." The children keep playing. "Johnny, Mommy said time to clean up." No response. "Johnny, did you hear Mommy? I said clean up right now." Nothing.

"Okay, Mommy is going to count to three and you better start to clean up. One. Two. Two and half. Two and—." You try a sterner tone. "Johnny, did you hear Mommy? I said clean up now. You know what? Mommy's going to help you."

You do a fine, practiced job of cleaning up. Finally, you put the train in the box. Johnny screams, "I want to keep that out."

"No, we are putting it away."

Johnny throws himself on the floor and screams until you say, "Okay, you can keep it . . . but just this once." (Right)

Lunch is an exact replica of breakfast.

You know you have to go to the store, which means you have to get ready, so you try to put Ash down for a nap. She refuses to cooperate. Not today, nor any day. She screams at the top of her lungs until, once again, you get her up saying, "Tomorrow you are going to take a nap!

Sure, Mom. Whatever you say.

After ten minutes, you are finally able to coax little Johnny to come upstairs and watch cartoons so you can quickly throw on some clothes and makeup. First, though, you must race around the room, putting all items they could get into out of reach. Future crises averted; you can get dressed.

There are interruptions, of course. Both Johnny and Ashley need something minute by ticking minute. You glance at your watch, finally ready to face the day. It's 1:30 in the afternoon.

Meanwhile, Ash has taken her poopy diaper off and is drawing something similar to a Picasso on the wall. Johnny has taken all your jewelry out of your case and has it spread out on the floor. It's your fault, of course. You forgot to put this up high where he couldn't reach it.

"Ashley, NO! You know better. Johnny, you know you shouldn't get into that." You spend the next thirty minutes cleaning up the disaster.

You go downstairs and pack up all the gear needed for the journey to the store. A thought occurs to you—before the wonderful days of raising kids, you would simply grab your purse, and you were off. Not now, of course.

A simple trip into town requires more supplies than are used to climb Mount Everest. You could survive two weeks in the desert on what has to go with you in the car. Diapers, wipes, binky, a spare binky, two bottles, formula, jar of food, water to mix the formula, snacks for Ashley, and some for Johnny, toys for each child, books for them just in case, favorite blanket and favorite stuffed animal for each child.

Johnny insists on having his own backpack with all his own stuff. You prepare a sippy cup with orange juice for Ashley, and you finally get the kids in the car. As you pull out, Johnny throws a fit because he wants to watch a *Thomas the Train* movie, not *Garfield*.

"Honey, Thomas is in the house. What about these other movies?" You list every kid's movie made since 1989.

"NO, I WANT THOMAS!!"

You put the car in park and run into the house to get Thomas. You put Thomas inside and Ashley begins to scream that she wants her sippy cup. You hand her the cup with orange juice in it. Oh no! She doesn't want the orange juice. She wants apple. Rather than confront her, you run into the house, get the proper drink, and now we are off to the store.

You get your two kids out, carrying your two-year-old and holding Johnny's hand. Johnny decides he wants to be carried, too.

"Honey, you are too heavy."

Not surprisingly, he throws a fit. You now have your purse, diaper bag, Johnny's bag, the sippy cup, and two kids in your arms, lugging them around the parking lot, frantically looking for a cart. The two-year-old begins to scream because the required binky was left in the car. You run back to get the binky, not wanting to risk any scarring.

The next step involves getting the kids into a shopping cart, but each child screams because they want the cart that looks like a car. You search another ten minutes, trying to find the one thing that will finally bring joy to your children. You find it and then you're off to get your groceries.

As you walk in, you notice that the evil people at *Walmart* placed the big candy display right at the entrance. Not wanting to battle with the kids, you fetch some candy for each.

As you begin to shop, little Johnny decides he has the sugar-fueled energy it takes to walk and wants out of the cart. You try and talk him out of it, but you can sense a small fit rising, so you pluck him from the cart. For the next thirty minutes you will say the phrase, "Johnny don't touch that" about a hundred times. You will take item after item from their hands and return them to the shelves.

Twice, Johnny gets mad and leaves, and you have to run to catch him. Both times, you say, "You better never do that again." In the toy aisle, a small mutiny begins when you say they couldn't get a particular toy. Finally, when enough people stop to stare at the writhing children, you say, "Okay, but just one toy."

Twice, Johnny has to go to the bathroom. You only have to change Ashley's diaper once—a small victory.

When you go to check out, you begin to notice the things you did not put in the basket but have magically appeared. Johnny insists on putting everything on the conveyer. You can hear the sighs behind you. Once again, evil *Walmart* has strategically placed candy at the checkout stand, knowing you don't have the strength to say no.

Back at the car, you load the groceries and the kids in the car. That's when Johnny says, "I want my toy."

Why didn't you take the toy out of the bag? You should have anticipated! You know the consequences of saying no, so you rummage through all the sacks until you find the toys.

Back home, you set the TV up and begin to put the groceries away. Your husband walks in with a big smile, kisses you, looks around says, "Where's dinner?"

Something inside your very soul snaps. You unleash hell. Stunned, your husband looks at you and says, "What got you in such a mood?"

This is the experience of many parents out there. If you're honest, you probably recognize elements of this story that are or have been part of your parenting.

God's Plan

I want you to understand that the scenario I just described is *not* God's plan. Parenting shouldn't be a burden. It should be a pleasure. You should enjoy your kids, and others should enjoy your kids as well. Let me quickly paint you a picture of what parenting *should* be. Some will say this is a fantasy. A fiction. But I can honestly say this is our experience with our children.

Imagine with me a world where your children did what you asked the first time, and they did it with a happy heart. You say, "Time to pick up your toys," and your children say, "Yes, Mom." Some of you would faint if that happened.

Imagine your kids, even at the age of one, are obeying your first request. Imagine not having to put everything up high so your eight-month-old doesn't get into it. You don't have to babyproof your house. Instead, you *house proof your child*. You can actually take your toddler to a friend's home, and they won't have to hide the remote and put all the breakables up. Your child will quietly play with the toys you brought.

This has been our experience.

Imagine a world where your teenagers enjoy the home and the family. They aren't trying to escape, aren't locked up in their room, alienated from you. They are still listening to your advice and doing what you ask. They are responsible. They talk respectfully to you and honor you. They still do what you ask, even if it isn't what they want to do. You can trust them out in the world. They are making good choices and decisions. They enjoy family time, hanging out with you. They seem to enjoy your company, and you enjoy theirs. Nearly every day blesses you with quality time you both enjoy.

Imagine a world where kids don't talk back to Mom, but honor and love their mom. (Yes, even in the teenage years.) No slamming doors when you ask them to do something. They are still saying, "Yes, Mom" and "Yes, Dad."

Imagine a world where you tell your two-year-old he can't have candy, and he is okay with that. No fits, no screaming. Imagine taking your three-year-old to a store and having no fits over toys.

Funny thing—kids raised with structure and love are happier than little Johnny. Johnny lives a life of getting what he wants. Our children will get what they *need*. Johnny is miserable; our kids are happy. Johnny will grow up thinking the world revolves around him (and will have a huge shock when he finds out it doesn't).

Our kids learn that they are a welcome part of the world, a world that loves them, but also expects to be loved back. They'll learn that life is better when it is about other people's needs, and that putting others before yourself makes for the best life.

Imagine a world where you can take your six-year-old, five-year-old, three-year-old and baby to a restaurant and have no fits, no screaming, but have people come up to you and say, "We were so scared when we saw you come in with all those little kids, but your kids are amazing." We have had this happen to us with our four boys and daughter. There are parents who can't take one three-year-old out to a restaurant because it is too embarrassing.

Imagine a world where your kids grow up and have a great relationship with you. They don't call you just on the holidays because they have to—they call you all the time because they *want* to. You are still able to share and be a part of their lives for as long as you live.

Imagine a world where your kids grew up and were successful in life. They were successful because you instilled character in them, for it's the character that you put in them that will shape your children's future.

Imagine a world where your kids were successful in school, work, and in their finances because you taught them how to have self-control, how not to give up, how to always give their best, and how to always do it with a happy heart.

Imagine a world where your grown-up kids loved God and were into church.

Imagine a world where your children have taken what you gave to them and carried it on from generation to generation.

Starting right now, you can begin to build this world. This can be the generation that is looked back upon as the one in which change happened. This is the generation where our kids got all that God wanted them to have out of life.

This world starts with you. I challenge you to build this world and change generations to come. This book—TRAIN UP A PARENT—will give you the tools you need to build this world.

Let's Finish This Book

Before we create this world, let's finish it.

Before you embark on the journey of parenting, I believe it is important to finish our children before we start. Let me explain.

Let's say you want to build the home of your dreams. You call up the builder and say, "Build us the home of our dreams."

He says, "What kind of house do you want, where should it be, how many rooms should it have?" "Oh, don't worry about the details. We just want a nice house."

Based on that scenario, I can guarantee you that you will *not* get the house you want. To build the home of your dreams, you have to *finish* the house first. Then you can build it. You have to draw out exactly how the house will look, where every window, door, even electrical outlets will go. Once the house is finished on paper, then you can start to build it. Finishing it is what determines what you need to do to get the house of your dreams.

Many parents enter parenting without knowing what they want to accomplish. They start to build their kids without ever finishing them. When you ask these parents what they want their kids to be like, they answer, "Well, we want them to grow up and be good." Easily done. I know good guys who are in their thirties who don't have a job or ambition in life.

"Well, we want our kids to be able to express themselves." The prisons are full of people who expressed themselves.

"We want our kids to love God." So, you'd really be happy if your grown-up child can't hold a job, can't stay in a relationship, is unmotivated in life, but loves to read the Bible and go to church? I, of course, love the parenting goal of, "We want the kids out of the house."

Then why did you have them?

It is impossible to know what to do if you don't know what you want in the end. Many parents fail at parenting, not because they do not want to be good parents, but because they don't *plan* to be great parents. Saying you want your kids to be good when they grow up is like me telling my builder I want a "nice house built."

Speaking of houses, I'll mention here that to say "I want my kids to love God" is like saying we want a good foundation on the house. More on that later.

Vision

Finishing really is just another word for vision. We need to have a vision for our children. Without a vision, our hopes and dreams for our children will perish. Vision is the most important part of parenting because it is the vision that guides you to the end result. The vision is what keeps you on track. The vision is what reminds you to keep doing what you are doing.

The Bible says that where there is no vision, people lack restraint. Vision brings boundaries and parameters into your life. When you don't have a vision, parenting becomes very inconsistent. One day your children can do something and that's fine. The next day, Mom goes off on the kids for the same thing. Without vision, it becomes very hard to give direction because you don't know in which direction you are going.

When your two-year-old child is throwing a fit in the store for candy, when you have vision, you know that giving in to tantrums now only makes your life harder later. You realize that if you can't control a two-year-old, you won't be able to control a fifteen-year-old.

Without vision, giving the child candy seems like the thing to do. The child stopped misbehaving, and everybody is happy— until the child doesn't get what she wants the next time. You find yourself raising a child that cannot control emotional outbursts. Once the child is grown, the adult can't hold a job because the boss won't give in to every demand. Marriage is tough because everything in the marriage needs to be about him, or he throws a fit. Life is tough because one day she finds out the world does not revolve around her. The world does not give in to tantrums.

Vision is what will help guide you along and will keep you on the path of great parenting.

We will start the book by casting the vision. We will start this book by finishing our children. Once they are finished, we can start.

The Goal of Parenting

Goal 1: The Ultimate Goal-relationships
We know parents who raised very successful kids. They were financially successful, successful in school and in their careers. Their kids grew up, moved out, and had little to do with Mom and Dad afterward—perhaps they called them on holidays. That, to me, is a failure in parenting.

We don't want to spend eighteen years raising our kids, giving our lives to them, and then have them move away and call us on holidays. Offspring who see us a few times a year only because it is the right thing to do.

The ultimate goal of the book is to develop a relationship with our children that one day turns into a great friendship, a friendship where our children look forward to seeing us, talking to us, and sharing their lives with us. They desire to be a part of our lives and want us in their lives.

Honoring us is not something they do because they have to, but because they want to. At four years old, they climb up on Mom's and Dad's lap and trust whatever we tell them. I want them to still come to us at forty years old with that same heart and attitude.

Our goal as parents is to have spent our lives building a trusting, loving relationship, that blossoms into a great friendship once the children are adults.

This vision is critical because it changes us. When you get up in the morning with that relationship on your mind, it changes how you respond and react to your children. It changes what you do and how you do it. When the relationship becomes the key factor, time with the children changes. There's a difference between spending time with the children and developing a relationship with the children. I know a lot of parents who "spent time" with the kids. Today, they have no relationship with them.

What's the difference between the two ways of looking at time? You could, for example, take your daughter to the park, sit on the bench and talk on the phone while she plays. You spent time with her. But what did you do to develop the relationship?

We need to stop being focused how much time we spend with the children and start focusing on how much relationship comes out of that time. This change in perspective changes everything. Instead of marking minutes, I'm at the park pushing my child on the swing, listening to her hopes and dreams. When relationship becomes a vision, it changes you.

It's this relationship that helps keep your children on the right track. There were things my older kid's friends were doing in high school—harmful things—that my kids might have done. But they wouldn't do those things because they knew it would break our hearts. It would hurt the relationship.

God created man for relationships. We were made to walk in love. That was God's plan. Inside of us is the need to love and to have great relationships. It's in our DNA. We will never feel the fulfillment, peace, joy, and happiness to the level our Creator intended for us until we are doing what we were created to do.

Relationships are the life blood of our emotions. When your relationships are going great, you are on top of the world. When they aren't going great, you are on the bottom.

Were Jesus asked to sum up the Bible, He might say, "Relationships. Love God, love others, love yourself." That is what the Bible is all about.

It is our job as parents to give our children the tools they need to have great relationships. It is our job to teach them how to love and what love is. Not the world's view of love, but *God's love.*

It is important to teach them the importance of trust, showing them that trust is the foundation of every relationship. Our relationships can never go beyond our level of trust.

We help them build a healthy self-esteem. Loving themselves is the key to loving God and others. We teach them how to share and how to give, but also how not to be taken advantage and how to set boundaries in their relationships. We teach them how to communicate and how to open up to others. Teach them how to create a life that naturally produces great relationships.

Goal 2: Character
We want our children to have Godly Character. We want Godly morals and virtues guiding their lives. We want them to have godly habits.

Most people think of habits as something bad, but habits can be a powerful positive force. Habits are important in raising kids. Habits are the key to the scripture, "Train up a child in the way he should go, and when he is old, he will not be able to depart from it." That scripture works because you instill habits, and when they're adults, they can't break that habit.

You instill the habit of loving others. They may want to be mean, but they can't because loving is a habit they can't break. You bless them with the habit of never giving up. They may want to quit, but that habit drives them to success. You put the habit in them of respecting authority, and though their friends are running wild, they won't because habit prevents them. They have a habit of being happy, thinking on good thoughts. They have the habit of forgiveness. Even when they are hurt and the other person is wrong and they want to hold onto bitterness, they won't because their good habit drives them to let it go. They have a habit of loving their siblings and parents, and when we make mistakes, and their siblings wrong them, they have no choice but to love them.

They have a habit of going to church. If friends want to go to the lake, they can't. They have been going to church their whole lives. Their family *has* got to go to church. This habit keeps them growing and changing throughout their lives.

You give them the habit of trusting in God, and though all those around them are stressed out, stress can't get a hold of your family, because that good habit keeps them in the peace of God and the joy of the Lord. Fear has no place in their lives, because of the habits we instill.

With this program, we will not be forcing morals onto our kids. Kids who have morals forced upon them are the ones who one day get into the most trouble. Instead, we will be instilling morals into them. Big difference. Many parents run a military camp, with all the don'ts in life. Those kids grow up always curious about all those don'ts. We put values, morals, and godly principles in their hearts. Positive habits will make up the character warehouse that will guide them into all of the great things that life has to offer.

Goal 3: Self-control
When you are out at restaurants, the mall or toy store, look around. How many kids lack self-control? They do not have the ability to sit quietly. They do not have the ability to control their emotions. They are emotionally driven.

That is not God's plan. Some are designated ADHD because they can't control themselves, can't focus, can't get themselves to sit still, can't control themselves to be quiet and courteous. Those kids grow up and can't keep a job because they can't get to work on time, can't work hard, can't focus on the task at hand. They can't finish school because they can't control themselves to go to bed at a reasonable time and can't get themselves to study. They cheat on their spouse because they lack the ability to control themselves. They destroy their lives because their parents did not teach them how to control themselves. They slip into depression because they allow their emotions to control their lives. The Bible says an emotionally driven life destroys itself.

When a child lacks self-control, he grows up with a life of doing whatever "feels right." Drugs feel right; being drunk feels right; dropping out feels right; an affair feels right. Our job as parents is to teach our children to do what is *right*, not what *feels right*.

The payoff is that if you do what is right, then you will feel right. Instant gratification destroys lives. Doing what is right builds a great life.

Parents today are not teaching their children self-control. We could take our two-year-old out to any restaurant and he would sit quietly and eat, and we could enjoy the meal. Why? Because we work hard at teaching and training our kids from birth how to control themselves.

Each of my kids threw a fit in a store one or two times. Then never again. Why? Because we taught them self-control.

The world wants to label your kids and drug them to keep them under control. ADD is a set of symptoms that describe a lack of self- control. The child cannot control himself for any appreciable period of time.

Self-control is something that is learned, not some God-given gift. Within each child is the ability to control himself. It is up to the parent to train him. Suppose your child has been diagnosed with ADD or ADHD. If you follow this program, Ritalin will *not* have to be a part of your child's life. In less than a year, your child will possess the skills needed to sit quietly, to listen, to have self-control. We have counseled hundreds of parents who have had great success with ADD.

Goal 4: We Enjoy Our Kids, And Others Enjoy Our Kids
Remember the scenario that opened this chapter? We can honestly say that Mom did not enjoy little Johnny or little Ashley. Nor would anyone else.

Did you ever have a kid come over to your house and misbehave? When he left, you probably thanked God and prayed he would never return? You wondered why that parent was allowed to procreate.

That is not God's plan. I don't care what are your kids are, they should bring pleasure wherever they go. You should be able to go out to eat without ruining everybody else's dinner with your screaming child. People should not have to listen to your kid's fit in the store. Babysitters should look forward to spending time with your kids. Your church should welcome them. School teachers should enjoy them.

I was in the toy store with my then two-year-old. There happened to be some other moms around with their kids also looking at toys. My Peyton said, "Mom, can I have this toy?"
And

I said, "No. We aren't getting a toy today."

Peyton said, "Okay."

Two moms turned to me and asked, "How did you do that? Is that a trick? Did you use magic? Do it again. We want to see it again."

Note that our parenting can be light to the world. When the world looks at successful Christian parenting, what they see are kids that are happier they are listening they are obedient. The world should ask, "What do you have that we don't have?"

We say, "Jesus." That testimony right there will get more people saved than 1,000 well-meaning but misdirected people on the street corner yelling, "You're going to burn in HELL."

What a joy it is when strangers comment on how great our kids are. This is the world *you* will create.

Notice by contrast how unhappy Johnny's mom was. What a horrible day! That is not God's plan—frustrated, mad, and upset! She couldn't get anything done. She probably went to bed feeling defeated, as if she'd failed.

The home is a better place when there are no fits or tantrums; where the kids do what they are asked to do and do it with a happy heart. You can build a relationship with your children in this type of home.

Johnny and Ashley's home will be a home of unhappiness, selfishness, rudeness, unkindness, frustration, and will end with two children who hate their parents.

Our home develops character, morals, and a relationship with our children that one day turns into a great friendship. We enjoy our children, and though we are proud of them, and when they grow up and move out, we miss having them around. Because as the Bible says, "When kids are raised right, they bring joy to their parents all of their days." (Scot paraphrased this, of course!)

Goal 5: Parent with Confidence
Have you ever been traveling someplace you've never been before? You might wonder whether or not you are going in the right direction. Maybe you missed the turn off, maybe not. You slow down, trying to get a clue where you are. After a while, you decide you did miss the turn off and you double back, wondering, "Maybe I didn't go far enough. Maybe I should turn around again." You spend time lost, going back and forth, wondering, questioning. So frustrating!

This is what happens to so many parents. They really don't know how to get where they want to go, so they spend their parenting days trying a direction, giving up, going another direction, giving up…

They try something and things don't look exactly right, and so they give up and try something else. Another parenting idea isn't working right away so they try something else.

What happens is you end up frustrating the child because he doesn't know what to expect. You are frustrated because you feel lost. And the behavior that bothers you gets worse if anything. If you don't have confidence in what you are doing, then you tend to give up on things that maybe are scriptural, but because you keep quitting or turning around, you never seem to get to the destination.

Since the God-given invention of GPS, traveling is so much different. I am going somewhere. Things don't look right' but the

GPS says we are headed in the right direction. GPS gives me the confidence to stick to it and to head toward my destination.

This program will be like a GPS in your life. When you finish, you will be able to step out confidently in your parenting. You will have a flow chart of what to do with different behaviors, and what you need to do to correct them. Things may not look right immediately, but as you continue on the path, you see you are headed in the right direction.

Before, you parented with fear. Now, you parent with confidence. And whether you know it or not, kids can sense fear and doubt. They can tell when you are easily swayed. The Bible says a double-minded man has no success in life. If you are double minded in your parenting, your kids will play you and keep you from the destination of great parenting.

Let me say that parenting out of fear is one of the worst things you can do. God did not give you a spirit of fear but of control, love, and a sound mind. Parents who parent out of fear lose control of their kids right away. They don't have the ability to love their children. The Bible says love and fear cannot live in the same place. Discipline, correction, direction is love. Fear keeps you from doing these things consistently. Fear will keep you from a sound mind.

Johnny's mom lacked a sound mind in many of her actions. She probably is a very intelligent person, but her fear kept her from acting like an intelligent parent. Fear will always prove out—what you fear will come true. A parent who has the fear of losing the love of his or her child will not discipline because, "What if they stop loving me?" (So sad because discipline done correctly strengthens the parent-child relationship.)

The undisciplined child gets whatever the child wants, not what the child *needs*. The child lives in this false world where everything revolves around him. The child grows up to be selfish and ungiving, and every time, in the teenage years, hates, (yes, I said *hates*) his parents. The fear of losing the child's love proved itself true.

After this book, you will know what to do as a parent. You will be confident that your children are going to be successful. They will marry the right person. They are going to attend church and have a close relationship with God. You will be confident that they are going to move towards their destiny.

You will be confident that you are developing a great relationship with your children that one day turns into a great friendship.

You will have that confidence because you will know that you are doing God's Word. You no longer are guessing as a parent, just rolling the dice and hoping for some change. Instead, you are stepping out confidently into your role as a parent.

Some Final Words—and Warning

If you were personally going to build your dream house, having never built one before, what is the first thing you would do? Get books on how to do it. You would study and study. You wouldn't just go out with a hammer and some nails and "figure it out as you go."

It is sad, but most parents raise children that way. They have a "we-will-figure-it-out-as-we-go" mentality. Their children reach their teenage years, and they realize, "We didn't have it figured out, and we have some real problems on our hands."

I challenge you to finish this program. Then in a year, go through the program again. The following year, become a leader in the program. Run this program out of your home or church.

Holly and I taught this class for twenty years. Each year, we were reminded of things we were not doing (even though we wrote it!). We discovered that must you listen to things going on in the season you are in. But seasons change. We get to junior high, teach the class and think, oh no, we forgot about that! Same thing for high school, and then we have another two-year-old, and oh man, we forgot about that. Great parenting takes wisdom and effort.

What is interesting is you will spend the time and do hard work one way or another. You choose whether or not you're successful. You can spend the time now teaching your kids, training your kids. Or later, spend time with the parole officer, the teachers, up all night wondering where the kids are. You choose how you spend the time.

It will seem like a lot of work because the old way seemed easier. Once again, you can do the hard work now or later. Yes, it is easier to give the kid a cookie at the store in the middle of a tantrum. It is easier to just clean up after them. It's easier not to make them do things the first time you ask. It is easier to just ignore your kids' actions when they are talking back to Mom. It's easier.

It gets harder in your child's teenage years, when their actions have consequence in the real world. It's a lot more work when the house is full of fighting and bickering. It's lot harder getting them off drugs, getting them bailed out, dealing with them not being able to keep a job, dealing with the DWI's, and dealing with them not wanting you in their lives.

I challenge you. Invest in life now and, in just six months, parenting will be so much better. It took a lot of work in the young years for us, but now it is so easy being a parent to great kids.

WARNING: IF YOU CAN'T GET A 3-YEAR-OLD TO LISTEN TO YOU AND OBEY, YOU WILL NEVER GET A 15-YEAR-OLD TO LISTEN AND OBEY…

CHAPTER 2:
A Child's Character Shapes His Destiny

Be careful of your thoughts,
For your thoughts become your words.
Be careful of your words,
For your words become your deeds.
Be careful of your deeds,
For your deeds become your habits.
Be careful of your habits,
For your habits become your character.
Be careful of your character,
For your character becomes your destiny.

Character is Your Children's Future

Your children's character will form, shape, and determine their adult lives. Whether they are successful in marriage or not is determined by the character instilled inside them. Whether they are successful in their jobs, in their finances, and successful with their own children is determined by their character. Character determines success in every area of life.

Your children's character will shape their future. Will their marriage work? Will they have great relationships? Will they be successful in business and finance? Will they be happy? Will life be great? All are determined by character.
Frank Pittman wrote, "The stability of our lives depends on our character. It is character, not passion, which keeps marriages together." Marriage is the perhaps biggest test of one's character, and without it, the marriage may not fare well.

It is character, not intelligence, which will bring success into your children's worlds. Walker Percy said, "People get all A's in school, and still flunk life." They were never taught perseverance, never taught what real love is. They don't know humility, so they are never, ever wrong, and people who are never wrong can never become better people. Sure, they're super-smart. Their parents made sure they worked hard at school. The problem is, they never worked on their character.

An old proverb said, "An ounce of character is worth a pound of intelligence."

It is character, not possessions, which brings joy to your life. It is character that can take you through life's storms and deliver you—happy, joyful, learning and growing—to the other side, where victory lives. It is character that creates your world and brings your destiny to your doorstep.

It is our responsibility as parents to raise up this generation of children with Godly character. You want great kids? The start, the end, and everything in-between has to do with character.

What is Character?

Character, in its simplest form, is what something is made of—the nature or the makeup of something. Our character is what is inside us. It's the thoughts and beliefs that inform your behavior; your inner qualities that set your action. It is what we are really like when no one is around. Who we are when no one is looking. What we are willing to do that no one can discover.

Character is the heart of man—that part with which God is concerned. God doesn't look at the outside. He looks at the intent of the heart. He looks at the character of man.

We, like God, will become concerned with the hearts of our children. It's not enough that your child did what you asked when you asked him to do the dishes because he stomped out of the room afterward, talking under his breath, and mad at you and the world. The action was good, but the child's heart was wrong. If we don't deal with the heart, the child will struggle through life. If we can set the proper character, good actions will follow.

The Levels of Character

What follows are the levels of character. Understand that each level builds on the previous level. We all start at Level 1. Our goal is to move our kids from Level 1 to Level 3. The success in their lives is determined by the level to which you take them.

Level 1: Give Me, Give Me
This is the level at which everyone begins. People who never move to the next level are people that do what *feels* right rather than what *is* right. They are more concerned about feeling good than doing good. They live on instant gratification. The world revolves around them, and when it doesn't, they fall into despair. An emotional tantrum will always follow.

This is where children start. They want their food *now*, want to be held *now*, want the toy *now*, want the candy *now*. If that's allowed, they will eat candy until they are sick.

At level 1, They want instant gratification with no regard to future consequences. Life and the world are all about them and what they want right. Fits and tantrums are part of the strategy for getting what they want.

The sad thing is, when parents don't train their children, their children stay at this level. You probably know adults who still throw adult tantrums, adult fits, have to get their way, go from one gratification to another, not caring who gets hurt. They are constantly sabotaging their future for instant gratification.

Children should be moving out of this level by age three to four. You should see some glimpses of them out of this level at age 2-3.

Level 2: The Chameleon or the Pharisee
Level 2 actually has two different ways your child will go. Both are fine as long as it is just a stage to getting to Level 3. Some children will go legalistic. Others will just adapt. Why? I don't know. I just know they need to get into it, and then get out of it.

The Chameleon
Adults stuck in this level have no firm set of values. Their character changes like the weather. These changes occur because the chameleon tries to please the people around them. Acceptance and approval determine their behavior more than any deep-seated internal sense of right and wrong.

At this level, your child will want to do right in order to avoid punishment. Doing the right thing is better than facing the consequences. For example, telling the truth is better than suffering the punishment attached to a lie. Unfortunately, the child isn't acting out of a love of doing right. Instead, they're afraid of being caught.

This is a normal stage—as long as we work towards the next stage. When the child is young, we lead them through the power of our authority. They behave because Mom and Dad said so.

When they get older, we lead our children through the strength of our *influence*. We train them to make good choices because it is the right thing to do.

It's very dangerous for a child to enter teenage years stuck at this level. Peer pressure is particularly strong, and the chameleon's need to please others can be a disaster.

Once again, many adults today are stuck at this level. What they believe isn't really based on internal values. In fact, chameleon adults don't know what they believe. They are the chameleons of character.

The Bible says that a double-minded man is unstable in all of his life (Scot paraphrasing here). They go from belief to belief, never able to move toward to the life God wishes for them.

The Pharisee
Some kids become all about the rules. This is the rule, and we can't break the rule. "Mom, what is the rule?" is a common question. In the younger years, these kids can be so easy to direct! Give them a rule and sit back. They'll not only follow, they'll make sure all around them are following along as well.

These are the children who say, "Mom, guess what Johnny did?" It is very important that we don't embrace this level and tell ourselves we have raised the perfect child. The pharisee child becomes a very annoying teenager and adult.

The one group of people Jesus had a hard time loving was adults stuck at this level. They elevated the *rule* above the *heart of the rule*. For example, "Do nothing on the Sabbath" was the rule. Jesus healed a man, and the pharisees were angry because he broke a rule—despite the fact that helping the man proved something about the character of Jesus.

The person stuck in the Pharisee level is the person who lives his life by external rules. Character is forced on them, so they do not develop their own sense of right and wrong. Doing what is right is a matter of obedience to the laws that have been established. They often take it upon themselves to be the voice of the law to all around them. They are judgmental, and very condemning.

Adults stuck in this level actually lack character because the context of the situation is never taken into account before they take action.

Here's an example: Grandpa takes weeks carving a car out of wood for a child. The child says that is ugly. It doesn't even look like a car. Reprimanded, the child says, "But, Mom, you said not to ever lie. It would be a lie to tell Grandpa I like it." The rule governs their lives, not character.

Yes, the child told the truth, following the letter of the rule. But character says you should look beyond the outside. You recognize what was put into the car—Grandpa's time and love. The child did not consider the heart of the gift. The Pharisees know all the rules, but they don't understand the *why* behind the rule.

You tell your child not to get out of bed. That is the rule. But if the child's sister gets sick in the night, I want to know about it. A child locked into the legalistic world might just sit in bed, following the rule.

The heart defines character—not mere obedience. It is vital, as we will discuss later, to teach our children the reason behind every rule, so they become governed by what's in them, not what is forced upon them.

Sadly, there are a lot of adults stuck at this level. These people lack character. They live in condemnation and in judgment. Their lives of living the rules keep them from being people of character.

Children will be in these stages from age two to fifteen. As they reach ages seven to nine, they should begin to demonstrate the characteristics of Level 3. Some of Level 2 will stick with them into their teen years—part of a natural growth process. Look for progress as they move on from Level 2. By ages fifteen to sixteen, they should be almost completely operating out of Level 3 character.

Level 3: Godly Character
These people have Godly morals, principles, values, and virtues inside of them. These will guide all of the choices they make in life. They understand the why's of the rules, and because of this, they look into each situation and find what they should do—not what the rule says to do. They don't do good just because they have to.

They do good because they *want* to. They have discovered that a good life starts with doing good.

They are able to see the value of people and act out of love and compassion. They understand the value of truth, and they seek out truth in love. They have self-control and do not do what *feels* right, but what *is* right.

This is our goal as parents. We will have kids entering into junior high and high school at this level. Our children's character in these years will catapult them into the successes of life.

Don't Skimp on the Ingredients

Character is made up of virtues. Virtues, in a sense, are the ingredients of character.

Though some ingredients might be more important, each ingredient is important for character to work in your child. For example, to bake a cake, I need flour, sugar, eggs, and milk. Now, if I tried to make a cake with just flour, sugar and milk, and decided eggs aren't that important, I would end up with a big mess. Many parents skimp on some virtues, and they end up with a teenaged mess. I implore you to make sure that you put all the ingredients of character into the hearts of your children.

My Kid is a Genius. No Wait, My Child Isn't that Smart

When talking about putting character into the hearts of your children, do not fall into, "They aren't old enough for that." It is funny to hear parents talk about how smart their kids are, but when it comes to correction, their kids' I.Q. drops drastically. The child is so smart, but at one year old is unable to keep their food on the table. Their child is a genius at seven months but can't learn the difference between a toy and an electrical outlet. This child is the smartest eighteen-month child ever but can't be taught "please" and "thank you." You can't have it both ways. Either they are smart, or they are not.

Understand this one thing; your children will rise to your level of expectation!!!

The funny thing about life? What you expect, you almost always get. It is interesting that the same is true in parenting. What you expect from your children, you will get from your children. If you expect that your children won't listen the first four times you call and won't respond until you blow your cork at them, then you'll find that they will wait for the explosion before responding. But if you expect your kids will respond the first time you call with, "Yes, Mom," or "Yes, Dad," the weirdest thing happens. They do.

Do your children go stomping through the house, slamming doors and talking under their breath about you? It happens this way because of what you expect. If you expect your kids to do what you ask the first time you ask it, and you expect them to do it with a happy heart, they will.

If a child of any age has to sleep in your room—or even worse, in your bed—you have to change your expectations. If your child can't go to sleep unless you sit in the room, you have to change your expectations. If your children are past the age of six months and freak out because they don't have their binky, you have to raise your expectations.

If your son is old enough to move around the room and you don't trust him not to touch everything, you have the wrong expectations. If the cupboards in your house are locked tighter than Fort Knox, you may want to change your expectations. If, on the other hand, you expect your child not to touch your remote and to stay out of the cupboards, they probably will.

What bewilders us are the parents that think their thirteen-month-old can't grasp the concept of don't touch. Yet they will likely brag about how smart and intelligent they are. Sorry, you can't have it both ways.

At one year, your children know what they can touch and not touch. They are very intelligent. They actually can be taught not to throw their food from the table, not to put it into their hair. They can actually be taught how to communicate, how to sign "please" and "thank you." My kids were saying "please" and "thank you" a year before they could actually say it.

Children under two years old can be taught first-time obedience. They can be taught the meaning of "no." They can be taught not to throw a tantrum. They can be taught how to play quietly. All it takes is the parents of these genius children to *raise their expectations.* What it boils down to is raising our expectations to God's expectations. Isaiah says if you have God's thoughts, you will have His ways. If you want God's ways with your children, then you have to have His thoughts on children. We have to get out of the "Dr. Spock, secular, let-the-kids-be-free, feed-their-every-desire" thinking, and raise our expectations within the home to a Godly level.

We raise our expectations to a Godly level, not lower them to a worldly level.

If It Feels Right, It Must Be Right

A while back, I was looking for something to watch on TV, and I happened to tune into a politically correct show—the kind where they get a bunch of nuts together and talk about how to morally destroy the earth. Their liberal views might even offend Satan on an occasion or two.

As I watched, the subject of morals came up. While discussing what our morals and standards should be, they came to an amazing conclusion. *If it feels right, then it must be right.*

If this is our standard for life—do what feels good—America is in trouble. This sort of thinking will destroy any life that adopts it. Such a life will be led by flesh and emotions. That life will never have any quality, long-lasting relationships. That life will never have a true sense of satisfaction, and will never have peace, real joy or happiness. It will be covered up by cheap thrills and ways to cover the pain that eats them up from the inside.

Understand that being a great husband may not always feel good. I don't always feel like talking to my wife. I don't always feel like putting her needs before mine. I don't always feel forgiving. I don't always feel like changing and being a better husband.

I don't always feel like putting on clean underwear, but I don't do what feels good. I do what is good. I don't do what *feels* right, I do what *is* right. Thanks to that, I have an amazing marriage that brings me joy and happiness.

To many men, the affair they had felt right. Watching another night of TV felt right. Ignoring the needs of their wives felt right. When they got done with what felt right, they were empty and alone.

Sometimes, being a great dad means putting down the remote and spending time with the kids. Sometimes that doesn't feel fun or convenient.

Sometimes I have to discipline. That definitely doesn't feel good. I have to make sure the kids honor and respect Mom.

I have to work to share their world, learn to get them to open up, talk to me, and share what is going on inside of them. I have to go to all their plays, sports, and activities. My life is about loving them and giving to them. Sometimes I don't want to do those things, but I do it because I do what is right. Because of that thinking, my relationship with my children brings me more joy, more peace, than a million NFL games or a million hours of mindless television.

Sometimes it doesn't feel good to work hard, be motivated, and excel. Sometimes it feels right to quit, give up. But we don't do what feels right. We do what is right.

This is the truth that we must plant in the hearts of our children. From the time they are born, we train them away from the thought of doing what feels right. Otherwise, they will destroy their lives, because:

- It feels good to smoke.
- It feels good to do recreational drugs.
- It feels good to have sex outside of marriage.
- It feels good to give up.
- It feels good to follow the crowd.
- It feels good to rebel against your parents.

Meanwhile:
- It doesn't feel good to abstain from drugs when all their friends are doing them.
- It doesn't feel good to have a curfew.
- It doesn't feel good to abstain from premarital sex.
- It doesn't feel good to study and do well in school.
- It doesn't always feel good to share and love their siblings.
- It doesn't feel good to obey their parents.
- It doesn't feel good to submit to their boss and work hard.
- It doesn't feel good to forgive and learn to let go.

We will not raise kids that do whatever feels good. Instead, we raise them to do the right thing.

To answer the politically incorrect question, what is the moral standard? It's easy. It is the Word of God. *That is the standard.* We, as parents, will raise our expectations to that standard. That is the level of our character training.

Raise the Kid to the Standard

This book is all about raising our kids with Godly virtues, Godly character, to a Godly moral standard. What many parents do instead is they lower the standard to the child.

Let's repeat that one more time because you may have just read over it. As parents, we should raise our kids to a Biblical standard. The problem is most parents lower the standard to the child.

They then give the child's sin a glorified name. They have cute little sayings for their child's lack of character. "He's all boy. She's just shy. He's a leader. She's very confident. He's got a lot of energy. He's outspoken." Let's look at each of these sayings and explore what they really mean.

For example, we are called to love others. That is the standard. There is no excuse not to do so. Suppose your child is at someone else's house, running through the rooms, roughhousing, being obnoxious. The host parent might say, "Well, he is just all boy."

No, he's not. He is annoying and rude. Being "all boy" does not give you or your child a pass to infringe on someone else's rights. All boy or not, that child needs to be raised to the standard. When we are at someone else's home, we think of them. We don't run. We are not loud. We do not touch things that should not be touched. That is the standard—our expectation.

Here's another example. We are called to love and respect others. That is the standard. Someone says, "Hi" to your five-year-old daughter, and she hides behind you and says nothing. "Oh, she is shy." You have just lowered the standard. She needs to say at the very least, "Hi," back. That is teaching her to come outside of herself and respect other people.

Suppose your three-year-old won't share and keeps taking toys away from the other kids. "Oh, he is just a leader." I have never heard John Maxwell call "not sharing" a leadership trait. Your child is not a leader. He is a selfish brat.

Your child keeps putting others down and bragging about what she can do that the other kids can't. The parent says, "She just has a lot of confidence." Actually, no, she doesn't. She has a very low self-esteem and only feels good when stepping on others. She lacks humility, one of the key character traits. And if you don't fix it, she will struggle all her life in relationships.

Do you have a daughter who gets all emotional and cries over everything that does not go her way? "You know girls are emotional." No, she's not emotional—she's spoiled. If you don't raise her to the standard, her life will be an emotional rollercoaster. There are circumstances where crying is acceptable. Not getting your way is not one of them. When she does something wrong and Dad is about to discipline her, she cries, and he says, "She's a girl. She feels really bad."

So, what's the standard? The Bible says, do not allow the tears of your children to keep you from discipline. The standard is, "The joy of the Lord is your strength," and "Rejoice in the Lord always. Again, I say, rejoice." Is it hard for you to discipline your children? "Count it all joy when problems arise, for they will build up your faith and get you to the place where you lack nothing." Those are just a few scriptures that set the standard. If she is allowed to be ruled by her emotions, she will have a very hard life (and her husband will have an even harder one).

Do you know a parent whose kid is totally out of control? "He just has so much energy," they say. Send him to my house for a week. I guarantee I can cut down his energy level. (There are always chores to be done!) He doesn't have too much energy—there are no standards in his life. He does whatever he wants. He lacks character.

Suppose Mom says to the three-year-old, "Please do this," and he says, "NO!" "Oh, he is just an outspoken little boy." No, he is a rude little child, who needs some Chapter 10 in his life. (You'll see.) Outspoken or not, the standard is to honor Mom. How will the boss react when the grown child tells him no? "He's just an outspoken employee?" Not a chance.

"Well, Scot and Holly, you don't understand. My kids are all different." Yes, they are, and that is great. All of my kids have different personalities. But understand, though personalities are different, *the standard always remains the same*. I may handle situations a little differently with each child, but they are each expected to rise up to a standard by which we as Andersons live.

People ask me, "Holly, you have all boys. Don't you have to allow them to be boys? They need to be rough and tumble a little bit." Sure, outside, but the standard in the house is, "We don't run in the house. We don't bounce balls in the house. We don't play basketball. We don't play hockey in my house. I like my house. It's pretty." What is amazing is that they do as we ask. And when we go to someone else's house, I don't have to give them a list of new rules. It is the same rules wherever we go.

Parent At Home for What You Expect in Public

One thing to get in this series is we parent at home for what we expect when we go out of the home. If your one-year-old isn't expected to sit in his chair and eat his food without throwing it all over the place, don't expect him to do it in a restaurant. If your two-year-old is allowed to roam around wherever he wants and touch anything he can get his hands on, don't expect anything different at someone else's house.

We parent at home for what we want when we go out of the home.

Standard In the Younger Years

Understand this; the standard you set in the younger years will determine whether the teenage years are fun or a lot of work, worry, and prayer. It will all be based on the standard you set.
You can cut the corners and do it the easy way. Suppose you ask your child to do something before school, but he didn't do it. Rather than go through the conflict later, you do it yourself and just let things slide. You hear your child mouth off a little bit to Mom, but you know that it's easier to ignore than to deal with the problem.

What you find is, all these little things you let slide make a huge problem when he's thirteen, fourteen, and fifteen years old. It is a whole lot harder to fix those things when they are older than when they are five and six years old.

Your craftsmanship in the younger years is going to show up in the older years. If you cut corners, it will cost you a lot more time and a lot more heartache later.

This Old House with Scot
In our last house, I was still in the "do-it-yourself" stage of life. I painted every room in that house, did my own wood floor, tile, most of the molding and crown molding in the house.

I, being an Anderson, did a lot of it the Anderson way, meaning I cut some corners. If you couldn't see it, I usually did not paint or trim it. So, in one room, we had this huge twelve-foot-by-nine-foot entertainment center. I painted the whole room, but I did not want to move the entertainment center, so I just painted right up to it, I did all the molding and trim right up to it. I painted our bedroom without moving the small entertainment center, and I only moved the bed enough so I could hide the white walls with color. I took the easy way out through the whole house.

We eventually sold the house and had to move. When all the furniture was out of the house, you could see and outline on the walls here everything had been. I wanted to work on my new house, but I had to spend two days doing paint, molding and trim in the old house. It would have been easier if I'd done things the right way, but instead, I had to play catch-up.

It's the same thing with your children. Problems are a whole lot easier to deal with it at four, five and six years old than to put parenting off and cut all the corners you can. And when they are fourteen, fifteen, and sixteen years old, your choices will come back and bite you.

Don't cut corners. Your kids will take every corner you give them because they are gamblers. They will take a chance on something if they think there are any odds at all of winning.

For example: If you sometimes ask your kids to do something three times and then get upset, and other days you expect them to listen the first time, they will *always* gamble in hopes of three. This makes life very frustrating to you, but also very frustrating for them. The Bible says, "Do not exasperate your children."

When you don't know what to expect, it is very frustrating.
How would you like to live in a world of inconsistent laws? Some days the speed limit is 50, and on other days, without you knowing, it is 35. "But, Officer, I thought it was 50."

The officer replies, "That is what is wrong with you. You don't listen to me. You don't care. No one in this city listens to me." Imagine that laws are just whatever the policeman is feeling that day! Some days he snaps for no real reason—he's been bottling up all the other laws being broken by his other children. Life would be so frustrating to you! Why? Because we need to know what is expected. We need consistency. Otherwise, we are exasperated in all that we do.

It's the same for your children. Deep down, they want consistent boundaries. They are happier when they know exactly what is expected. If the expectation is first-time obedience, they never have to guess, never have to wonder if Mom will go off on request number three or four. The standard is first-time obedience, with a happy heart. "Okay I can do that."

But if you are not consistent, if you give them just a little, they will always take a little more. If you give a mouse a cookie, he will want a glass of milk. If you will give him ten percent, he will try for fifteen percent to see how much you give him.

This happened with every one of my children when he was around fourteen months old. He had a sippy cup with a drink in it. I say, "The cup stays on the tile floor in the kitchen."

Now, every single child on earth will try to take one step onto the carpet. Just one toe, right? They are saying, "Come on, Dad. Give me 10 percent." I know a lot of parents who would say, "Well, he is pretty much on the tile. I don't want to do battle over that."

What happens when he is fifteen, sixteen years old and the curfew is at 11:00 pm and he comes in at about 11:45 pm? You see, he continues to take the extra for the rest of his life. I don't want to raise a child who is "barely over the line" on everything in life. Each of my children put a toe on the carpet just once, and guess what? I never had to deal with it again.

Pastor, that's such a little thing. Why make a big deal out of it? Because that 10 or 15 percent has a chance of destroying their lives in the teenage years. I'm not willing to risk that.

When Dad says, "Don't hang out with those friends," he'll sneak away and ditch a class, just to put his toes over. He will do just enough and get his little toes over the line because Dad did not take the time with him when he was two years old. That's unacceptable. I am not going to accept anything but 100 percent from my children. That is the standard.

When I ask you to do something, you don't do a 90 percent job and stomp your feet all over the house, pouting and mad. Because if I allow that then, when you become an adult and your boss asks you to do something, your attitude and 90 percent will get you fired.

The Bible says, "Give no foothold to the devil." To properly picture this, imagine you are in a room and the door needs to be closed but you leave it just an inch open, and Satan gets his little foot in that opening. It is nearly impossible to close that door with a foot in it. Many adults struggle because they give Satan that little foothold into their lives. Then, it's too hard to close that door. I won't allow that into my child's life.

I leave you with this thought. If you can't get your three-year-old to listen and obey, what in the world makes you think your fourteen-year-old will? If you can't get your child to listen to you when they are right in front of you, what makes you think they will listen when they are off at school? Raise your kids to the standard. Stop lowering the standard to the children.

Warning: It will be hard to set certain new standards in the home until we have done some later chapters on discipline. In the meantime, explain the new standard to the kids, then explain how you are going to be practicing this standard for the next few weeks. Make a game out of it. Ask the children to do something. If they don't, remind them of the game and let them know in a few weeks there will be a consequence for not doing as asked. Please do not do any new discipline in the home until we have taught you the right way. Discipline done right will change their direction. Done wrong, it does more damage than not doing it all.

Questions for Review:

1. What is character to you?

2. What are the three levels of character?

3. At which level of character are your kids now? Explain why they are at that level. Are you seeing any Level 3 character traits? If so, explain.

This week at home:

Be prepared to share with your group a new standard (expectation) in the home that you set. How did the game work with the kids?

Be honest. Is there a standard you lowered as a parent, and did you give it a cute name? ("Oh, he is such a leader.")

Homework for Dad and Mom:

Read chapters 2 & 3 of *More Than a Dad/More than a Mom*.

CHAPTER 3:
A Great Life Starts with Wisdom and Understanding

There are ten virtues or ingredients we need to put into our children. Let's take a close look at each of them. In this chapter, we'll begin with what may be the most important.

Virtue 1: Wisdom and Understanding

The Greeks considered wisdom to be the master virtue, the one that directs all the others. I would argue the Bible also puts it at or near the top. Wisdom is good judgment; the ability to make right choices. Wisdom enables us to make right choices at the right time for the right reasons. Wisdom tells us how to put all the other virtues into practice, when to act, how to act, and when to disregard one virtue for another that is more important. For example: Not telling the truth because it would hurt someone's feelings. When the wife says, "Does this dress make me look fat?" a husband of character says, "No" (rather than tell the truth and say, "The dress doesn't make you look fat. It's your hips.")

The Bible talks about having wisdom and understanding. It is important that we know the difference. Wisdom enables us to discern correctly to see what is truly important in life, and to set priorities. Understanding allows us to use wisdom in an infinite number of situations. Understanding keeps us out of legalism, where the rule is elevated above the reason behind the rule. Understanding tells us why something is right, and why something is wrong. We understand not just what to do, but *why* we do it.

The wisest man ever has some thoughts on Wisdom.

Proverbs 3:13-18
13 Happy is the man who finds wisdom, And the man who gains understanding.
14 For her proceeds are better than the profits of silver, And her gain than fine gold.
15 She is more precious than rubies, And all the things you may desire cannot compare with her.
16 Length of days is in her right hand, in her left-hand riches and honor.17 Her ways are ways of pleasantness, And all her paths are peace.18 She is a tree of life to those who take hold of her, And happy are all who retain her.

The Bible says one of the most important things you can teach your children is wisdom and understanding. Nothing you teach can compare. It's great you taught your son how to throw the ball so he could be successful on the team, but did you teach him wisdom so he could be successful in life? It's great you taught your daughter how to use makeup to interest the boys, but did you give her wisdom, so she makes right choices in the relationship?

With wisdom comes a long life, blessings, honor, peace, joy, and happiness. There is no greater gift you could give to your children than to give them wisdom and understanding.
Wisdom and understanding will equip your children so that they can make right choices in life. If they make right choices, they will have a great life.

Choice Determines Life

Deuteronomy 30:19 (New King James Version)
19 I call heaven and earth as witnesses today against you, that I have set before you life and death, blessing and cursing; therefore choose life, that both you and your descendants may live.

I call heaven and earth as witnesses today against you, that I have set before you life and death, blessing and cursing; therefore choose life, that both you and your descendants may live.

Life is about choices. Make good choices and you will have a good life. Make bad choices; you will have a bad life.

God says that what lies before your children is a great life and a not-so-great life. You choose. It is like a multiple-choice test. What makes it so easy is, He gives you the answer. He says, "Choose life."

Wisdom and understanding will help your children choose right friends, choose to do good in school, choose to respect authority, choose the right spouse, choose to walk in love, choose to forgive, choose to work hard, choose never to give up, choose to be a good spouse, choose to be a great parent.

We will set them up for a successful life, a life where they are constantly choosing life. It will be habit inside of them, where they choose right without even thinking about it. Good choices just flow out of them. Out of the good treasures in their hearts come great things. This character habit will have no choice but to produce a great, successful life.

As parents, one of the most important things we can do for our kids is to equip them so that by the time they are thirteen, fourteen, or fifteen years old, they make good choices from the heart and do what is right. And they do right, not because they are afraid, they are going to get in trouble, but because they want to do right.

In the early years, it's the consequences that help them make right choices, but there is an important transition where they start to make right choices because they *want* to do so. We transition them from Level 1 character to Level 3 character. This, parents, is our biggest job. It's getting the right things in them, so that later in life, the right things will come out of them. We're not forcing rules down their throats. We're instilling Godly principles into their hearts. As parents, we'll spend a majority of our time working on the inside of our children and getting that heart of theirs ready to choose life.

What Guides Us in Our Decision Making?

I want you to picture a huge warehouse. Inside this warehouse is everything you have learned in life. All that you believe to be true is stored here. It is your Wisdom Warehouse. The purpose of this warehouse is to help you make better choices in life.

Now, every time a decision is going to be made, what I will call a little man (your conscience) goes down to the warehouse to see if there is any information to help you make a decision.

For example: You go to Wendy's and pay for your meal and the cashier gives you $10 too much change. A decision needs to be made. The little man goes down to your warehouse and looks for information on this. For some, he will come back and say, "You know what? This is a lot like stealing. The poor girl will have to pay back the money. I think you should let her know." Having been advised, you make a choice based on this information.

For others, the little man goes down, comes back up and says, "It's yours. It is a blessing from God. The wealth of the wicked is laid up for you, my friend. I think you should keep it and buy some weed." (The weed part may not be for all.)

Having been advised, you make a choice. If you go along with his advice, he rewards you. You give the money back, and you feel good inside. You did right. Maybe the voice said, "Give it back," and you decided to keep it. You might realize there is an emptiness inside of you. You feel guilty and bad. Your conscience is punishing you, trying to get you to do what it believes to be right. Finally, you return to Wendy's and give the money back. Suddenly, you feel great.

The Job Description of Your Conscience

First, your conscience lets you know what is in your Wisdom Warehouse for any situation requiring a decision. It may warn you if you are about to do something it believes to be wrong, or it may prompt you to do something right. Sometimes there's no advice at all because there is nothing in the warehouse concerning the choice at hand.

Second, your conscience has the job of trying to make you follow the Wisdom Warehouse's suggestion. Your conscience will reward you for following through. If you ignore the advice, it will accuse you (using guilt as a last-ditch effort to get you to do what it believes is right).

Now, if you continue to not listen to your conscience, one day the little man will give up. He gets hardened. That is a very bad place to be. In a way, you have shut down your decision-maker. Mass murderers feel no remorse, nothing. What happened? After years of ignoring the conscience, it just shuts off.

The Wisdom Warehouse helps you make decisions. I think it is interesting that you could have the same scenario, but different people come up with different responses from their little man. You see, *the warehouse is only as good as the amount of wisdom that is put into it.*

Let's look at an example. Your boss has just left work, and you are unsupervised. You think, "I should play some angry birds." You have a choice to make. For some, the man comes back and says, "We need to work hard. Work shows good character. Work if you want that promotion, work if you want to get ahead. I think you should work." For some, the man comes back and says, "Everybody else is goofing off. This is a gift from God. Relax, enjoy. Let's get some weed. (The weed part is not for all.)

Let's look at another example. A woman is flirting with you at work. Some hear a voice that says, "You better run. This could be a lot of trouble. This could ruin your marriage." For others, the voice says, "Go get it. Maybe later we can get some weed. (The weed part is not for all.)

All of this happens in a matter of a second. Most of the time you don't even realize this is going on. Your life is running on cruise control. Unfortunately, a lot of people have the cruise control set on destruction. They wonder why they can't get ahead, why relationships constantly fail, why they can't keep a job, why nothing in life goes right. It's because, subconsciously, they are choosing death. They lack the wisdom to make good decisions, or the self-control (next chapter) to listen to their conscience.

The quality of life is determined by the quality of decisions you make. The quality of decisions is determined by how much wisdom is in you.

Our job as parents is to instill wisdom in our children. We want to get as much in their warehouse as possible so they can make good decisions in life.

Kids Are Born Good?

Some say that humans are born with a full warehouse, and it is society that corrupts it. These people are smoking something. They want to say, "Kids are born with goodness in them." Whoever said that never had a kid. People say, "Kids are just so pure, so innocent." They say we teach them our wicked ways.

Really? Because I know for a fact, I never taught my one-and-a-half-year-old to bite when someone takes his toy. I never taught him to scream when he doesn't get his way. I want to know who taught my child to lie almost at the same time he learned to speak. The Bible says we were born in sin. Wrong comes *so* easy. You could put a couple of babies on a deserted island, and they would, without any help, teach themselves how to be hurtful, how to be mean, how to be selfish (and even how to grow weed). Those things come naturally.

Our job is to teach them how to do right. We do that by filling up their warehouse.

It Starts with Us

Training our kids starts with us. Our kids' warehouse will reflect ours. Our values, what we really believe, will get to them one way or the other.

Let me explain. Their warehouse isn't being filled just by what you *say*. It is affected even more by what they see you *do*. You say, "Smoking will kill you. Don't do it." But they see you puffing on that cigarette. You say, "Lying is wrong," but you lie on the phone all the time. You say, "Don't give up," but they watch you give up. You tell them, "Love is being kind," yet you are mean to their mom.

Understand this. Men, your sons are learning what love is, based on how you love their mom. Your daughters are learning what to expect from a man based on what you give to Mom. The kids are watching. They are learning. The warehouse is being filled more by what they see than by what they hear.

It is vital that we walk the walk, that we to are living a biblically based life. It never seems to work telling your kids to do what I say, don't do what I do.

Parents: Huge Warning!

It is very important that we put right things into that warehouse. Wrong things can greatly hinder their choices. That's why it is so important that we continue to read books, read the Bible and go to a church that helps us change and get better.

Be careful to make sure we put the Word of God in them and not religion. Religion is a bunch of man-made rules forced upon people. God's principles are based on love

People's lives have been ruined because religion got into their warehouse. For example, early on, we went to a church where it was a sin for a woman to wear pants. My mom felt guilty one day for working in the garden in her blue jeans. She thought, "Oh, my God, I am sinning?" Was she sinning? No, but she still felt guilty. Arbitrary rules were inhibiting her decision-making.

The wrong information put into children's consciences can carry over into adulthood. The church told me at age five, "If you lie, you go to hell." Well, as luck would have it, I had already lied by then. I had lied so much, I figured I would be running the underworld. I was going to hell. This thought drove me crazy for almost a year, until one night, I went crying to my dad, saying I was going to hell. Worse, during that year I thought, "Why tell the truth? I'm already burning in hell."

Religion can make you feel guilty about everything. Before long, you realize, "I can't live up to this. This guilt will drive me insane." Finally, you quit Christianity and dive right into the world.

Don't get dragged into dumb rules. Things that in your gut just don't make sense. Why can't a woman wear pants? Why can't we play cards? As Jesus taught, life is about loving other people. We teach to share, to be kind, to encourage, to speak positive, and make others feel important.

The Key to Wisdom, UNDERSTANDING!

It is very important that we know wisdom and have wisdom in us, so we can put it into our children. But what is equally important is that we put understanding into them also. Wisdom without understanding is just a list of rules that never really can guide our decision making.

For example, your dad says stealing money is wrong. That wisdom is put inside of you. Then, the cashier at Wendy's gives you too much money. You didn't *take* the money. It was *given* to you. In that case, you were never given understanding of stealing is. You couldn't transfer the concept of stealing money to different situations. Understanding says, "Yes, she gave you the money, but you are still taking something that is not yours. That lacks character."

Wisdom is very specific. "Don't take your sister's toy." But that doesn't mean I can't take my friend's toy, right? Understanding says, "Don't take from others." Understanding makes it so you don't have to give your children one trillion different points of wisdom. One point of wisdom with understanding can cover a multitude of situations.

Understanding, in its simplest form, is the *why* of things. If a child can understand why something is right or wrong, he can transfer that wisdom over to an infinite number of situations.
You give your child the "don't" and you have covered just that particular situation. If you give them the why, you have covered all similar situations. Don't is just a way to control a child on the outside. The why allows the child to control himself from the inside. The why is the key. It is the KEY part of moving your child to Level 3 character. It is the KEY to a successful life.

Wisdom and Understanding Training

Let's look at an example. You've told your child not to "run in the house."

This timeless piece of knowledge is logged into the child's warehouse, and when running in the house comes up again, he has something to draw from.

But what about understanding? Suppose you explained how the house has a lot of nice things in it that could get broken? "Mom has spent a lot of money and time making the stuff in this house look nice. It wouldn't be nice if you broke something that was important to Mom. It wouldn't be right for Mom to go out and break your steering wheel off your bike. How would that make you feel? Plus, you could run into someone and hurt them. Running is for outside or in a gym, a place where you can't ruin someone else's nice things or hurt someone."

Two weeks later, you are at the church and some kids start running. Your child's warehouse of wisdom says, "Nothing down here about running in a church. Go for it. Hey, look. There's some weed. (Weed doesn't apply to all situations.)

But the child with understanding knows the *why* of things. When faced with running in the church, the little man comes back and says, "There are a lot of nice things in here. We could bump into someone and hurt them. This isn't a gym. I don't think we should run."

In both cases, the child knows that running in the house is against the rules. Without understanding, you'll require a number of subsequent rules. "Don't run in church," and "Don't run in your grandparent's house," and "Don't run in the china shop."

With understanding, the child can apply the wisdom to multiple situations.

Here's another example. Your child invites a friend to your home. You notice your son isn't sharing. You say, "Johnny, let Timmy have a turn with that truck." Not much to log in the warehouse. No learning happened, so next week, when another friend is over, Johnny is still hogging the toys.

What if, after Timmy leaves, you explain about sharing and how it makes friends. How would Johnny feel if he were at Timmy's, and Timmy did the same thing to him?

The next time Johnny has a playdate, there's something in his warehouse to help him make a better choice.

Now, this doesn't mean he will always make the right choice, but that conscience will make him feel guilty. If you reinforce the wisdom and understanding by building him up when he does share, and reminding him when he doesn't, you will soon have a child making good sharing choice.

Here's another example. You catch your child saying mean things to his brother. You say, "You can't talk to your brother that way." Once again, hardly anything was put in the warehouse. Not much to draw on at school with other kids.

What if you gave him the *why* of being nice and using nice words. Explain how he would feel, how it hurts the other person's feelings. Explain how building people up even makes you feel better.

Once again, whether in school or in the neighborhood, his warehouse has something to give to him.

I remember as a child the way my dad gave me the why's and how it stuck with me. I was about four or five. Dad had two baked potatoes. Dad said, "Which one would you like, the big one or the little one?"

As a child, I said, "I want the big one, Dad."

He answered, "Son, let me talk to you a little bit about what you do when you pick first, because there is somebody who goes second. You want to love them, so you pick the smaller one so that the other person can get the bigger one."

For some reason, that wedged itself inside my heart.

Fast-forward to when my kids were four and five years old, and I had two cookies of different sizes. I was so excited! A trainable moment! I would be able to train my kids. So, I called out, "Kids, Dad has cookies." They came running. I said, "Laken, which cookie do you want?"

He naturally said he wanted the big one—naturally—so I said, "Son, when we get to pick first, we want to pick the little one because we want the person that goes behind us to feel loved." And I began to share all the things that my dad shared with me. With a big proud smile on my face, I repeated, "Which cookie do you want?"

And he said, "I want the big one."

I said, "No, Son, remember what I said." I reiterated the main points and asked again, "Which cookie do you want?"

"Dad, I still want the big one."

"Son, which cookie would Jesus pick?"

He thought for a moment and said, "Jesus is very big. He would pick the big cookie."

I said, "No! No! No! Here's a new rule for you. WHOEVER PICKS FIRST FOR THE REST OF YOUR LIFE, THEY WILL PICK THE SMALLER ONE OR THEY WILL BE IN A LOT OF TROUBLE!!!!

I said, "Laken, which cookie do you want?"

He thought for a moment and smiled. "Why don't we let Heath pick first?"

We All Need the Why's

One thing I want you to understand is we all like the whys. When we get the why as adults, it helps us choose better. When we are just told to do something because someone said so, the natural reaction is to do the opposite.

Suppose you are at my church, and I say to a group of you, "Don't touch that wall back there."

Some of you may ask, "Why?"

I say, "Because I told you not to."

Inside of most of you rises the thought, "Who does he think he is? Don't touch the wall? I'll touch the wall if I want to. No pastor is going to tell me what to do." How many of you would touch the wall anyway?

But if I said, "Hey, don't touch the wall back there. We just painted it, and if you touch it, you'll get wet paint on you, and we'll have to repaint it."

Most of you would not want to touch it. Of course, you always have the few who still want to touch it. But for most, the *why* was enough.

When we give our children the why, it helps them understand how some things are right and others wrong. If your children are going to ever get to the place where they govern themselves, this is important. They start to do right because inside they believe it is right.

Children who are just given rules are governed by outside rules forced upon them. They will never move past Level 2 character. They resent the rules and desperately want to break out of their

moral prison. Children who understand why things are right and wrong have been given the tools they need to transition into adulthood. They are able to tie all the lessons on
sharing and being nice, talking nice and not stealing into really loving others, giving to others, or being a great spouse. Their warehouse is complete. Kids with rules along struggle in their adult lives, constantly confused, living in guilt, in shame.

How To Do the Why

Number One: At What Age Does the Why Apply
The why doesn't start to make sense to children until they are around four years old. Before that, they cannot really reason out what you are saying and place it in that warehouse. I am amazed to see a parent reasoning with a two-year-old throwing a fit. "Sweetie, we can't get candy because it is bad for your teeth to get candy. Mommy knows you want the candy, but it isn't healthy for you." A two-year-old will still scream, of course. "Okay, Sweetie, this time we will get the candy but next time, no."

Come on. A simple, "We aren't getting candy today," should be fine. The child cannot reason at that age. Now, just because they don't understand the why until they are four doesn't mean we wait until then. I start the why right away. *Not for them, but for me.* It gets me in the habit. It helps me build the skill of the why.

This is different from reasoning with them like the lady with the candy. I say, "No," I mean, "No," and then I may give the why. We aren't negotiating the morals at this time. That comes later. In the meantime? Practice.

Number Two: The Why is a Privilege!
The why is a privilege, not a requirement for obedience. There are times my kids do what I ask because I say so. I don't have time for the why at that moment and I just need them to do it. If your children can't obey without the why, then they don't get the why until they can oblige. The why is a privilege. This keeps you from

falling into the rebellious *why dance*—a strategy where everything in life is a why.

"Finish your food." "Why?"
"Clean up your plate." "Why?"
"Time for bed." "Why?"

This is a form of rebellion. (You will learn how to deal with this later. For now, "Because I say so," is fine.) The child obeys because you spoke. You give the why's in situations that require it.

For example, "Finish your food," doesn't need a moral explanation. In addition, children do not get to demand the why for obedience. When you obey, you then get the why. Obedience is first.

Now, there are times the kid sincerely asks why. You can tell that they really want to know. Those are some of the best teachable moments. Their heart is open and wanting some understanding. You'll know the difference between sincere interest and rebellion. (When I get the rebellious why, "Because I said so," is always the answer.)

There are three types of why questions.
1. *The why of curiosity.* "Why do birds have wings and we don't?" This is a great relationship-building time, where you speak into their heart.
2. *The why of morals.* "Why do we tell the truth?" This is a great time to build understanding.
3. *The why of challenge.* "Why do I have to?" This is rebellion and needs correction.

Number Three: Try to Focus on the Good
Reinforcing your kid's behavior when they do right has a much bigger impact than disciplining when they do wrong. We as parents can get so caught up in all the don'ts, we miss when they do the dos. We see when they don't share, but we don't see when they

give. We see when they are mean, but we missed when they truly had a heart of kindness. We need to open our eyes up and begin to elevate the good; really appreciate them when they do right. That feeling of Mom and Dad being proud will keep them motivated to do right. This will be the driving force getting them to Level 3 character.

We transition from mostly negative training to mostly positive training. If we do not, we limit the child's ability to reason morally. They get so caught up in the don'ts in life that they can't see the dos.

When our children are teenagers, I don't want them to abstain from something because they are afraid that they are going to get caught, or because they're afraid of the consequences. I want them to do right because it is the right thing to do; because it feels good inside to obey and do what we placed in their hearts.

Meanwhile, in the early years, (we get more into this later), it's the consequences that keep them from doing wrong. But there is a very important transition phase, and you want them to transition into doing it because it's good. That is why it is vital that we praise and esteem the good things our kids do. We don't just punish the bad. We reward the good.

For Baylor's sixth birthday, he (of course) got more toys from the grandparents than I got my entire life. These were the people who gave me a trash can for Christmas, and they just bought out the west wing of Toys 'R' Us.

While opening the gifts, he found a Batman plane. Right away you could tell Laken was into this. Laken said, "Baylor, I will open this for you and put it together." Sure enough, he put it together, got all the stickers on it, played with it all day.

About a week later, Grandma came over to take Baylor out for Grandma time (when she takes each child out by himself to build relationships). Come to find out, they went to the toy store. Baylor and Grandma came into the house. I said, "Baylor, what did you get?"

He pulled out the exact same Batman plane. I said, "Son, you already have that plane. Did you lose it?"

He said, "No."

I said, "Baylor, is your plane broke?"

He said, "No, Dad. I didn't get this for me. I got it for Laken." That right there was one of my greatest moments of being a parent. I praised Baylor for weeks in front of everyone with whom we came into contact. I elevated the good. Baylor got more joy out of that act of kindness then he would have ever gotten from any toy.

We, as parents, need to look for the good. Look for your children to be nice. Look for them to share. Look for them to do an act of kindness on their own. Then, praise them. Reward them with your words, but even more important, praise them in front of others. It is one thing to get a pat on the back in private, but it is so much more to get it in front of other people.

Number Four: Don't Be a Pharisee.
Children who grow up in a legalistic home will develop a hardened conscience. They will never, never move past Level 2 character. They will turn off their choice maker.

Legalism in a nutshell is where everything is black or white, wrong or right. There is no grey in life. The rules are elevated above the principle. The rules, in a way, become a God in their lives. The rule becomes more important than doing what is right.

I love what Jesus said in Mark 2. The rule is for you, not you for the rule. He was discussing the sabbath. God gave man the sabbath, a day to rest, relax, do whatever you want on that day.

Man, in a legalistic fashion, taints this. You can't turn on the oven; that is work. (I got this nugget of information from a Jewish man.) What if you love to garden? You can't work in your garden. The blessing becomes a burden. They missed the heart of the rule. Have a good day and do whatever you want. *It's your day.* But the rule subverts this, telling us what we can and can't do.

Context - Look into the Situation
Context means we look into the situation and use common sense and good judgment to find out what a person of good character would do. Often times, you have to look beyond a rule, look at the heart or reason for the rule, and then not do the rule because it is the right thing to do.

The rule was not to do much of anything on the Sabbath. When that rule was made, healing a sick man was not the reason for the rule. When they wrote the rule, there is no way they could write down all the conditions for when you could break the rule. If someone breaks into your house on the Sabbath, do you let them take your wife and kids? You have to take the context of the situation into account and make a good judgment. That is true wisdom and understanding. Jesus said a man being healed is not what the rule wanted to limit. The right thing to do was to heal the man.

Legalism says, "No. Right is right. Wrong is wrong." We do not want to raise our kids like this. We need to first demonstrate context as a parent, and then also teach it to our children. Show them that sometimes, having good character means breaking the rule.

We allow our kids to explain why they did what they did. We hear their hearts, look into the situation and find out if breaking the rule was the right thing to do. We cannot be rule-driven. We are character-driven. If the child made the wrong decision, we explain why what he did was still wrong. (If he is just making up some silly excuse to get out of trouble, you'll know it, and they know that they were wrong. Then we deal with that.)

I remember watching a movie when I was teenager. I don't remember the name, but the plot sticks with me today. The man was a very religious man. The bad guys had his family. Because of his religious beliefs, the man could not lie. They asked where his wife was, and he had to tell them because lying was not an option. He died. His wife died. The rule of lying was elevated above the life of his wife. The rule was more important than doing what was right.

You tell your child never to hit someone. In a legalistic world, if he were being attacked by another kid or witnessed a kid beating up a girl, there would be nothing he could do because the rule is more important than doing what is right. No, you don't hit others unless you are protecting yourself. You protect others. You can stand up for yourself. The why of things helps us protect against legalism.

We need to be like Jesus who defied the rules of the day (like you can't heal on the Sabbath). The rule was more important than doing what was right. What did Jesus hate? He hated legalism. He hated the rule that kept people from doing what was right. The rule should never keep one from having great character.

If your kids can't do something, and you have no reason why, you really need to reconsider your decision. Legalism often doesn't have a why. There is no real good reason for the rule. This can exasperate children, make them want to rebel, and get out from under this legalistic oppression. It hardens their hearts and their conscience. In the end, it can do the opposite of what you wanted. It can catapult them into all the things of which you were afraid.

Legalism tries to wall off your kids from the world with rules. What happens is, your children grow up in this over-protective cage, wondering what is on the other side of that wall. Sometime in their teen years, they jump over that wall and go nuts in the world.

We don't build a wall around our kids from the world. We suit them up so they can be a light to the world. Jesus says we live *in* the world, not *of* it. We put the principles in their hearts so they can go and function in their jobs, function in life, and be a light.

Suppose you hear, "Hey, they were cussing at work, and I just quit. I showed them." Showed them what? That Christians are weird? A little cussing hurts you so much? What if you stayed there and worked hard, allowed them to see what a great life you have, let them see your love and kindness. You don't judge them. Instead, you do like Jesus did—love them. Jesus didn't go hang out in the synagogue with the rule-makers. He was a light to the sinners.

Parents embarrass their kids by pulling them out of class because they are teaching evolution. If your child's Christianity is so shallow that teaching that we come from monkeys can turn them to Darwinism, you have bigger problems than evolution.

"We don't do Halloween." Why? "Because it is Satan's day." What are you talking about? *Every day belongs to God.* I refuse to give Satan a day. You have Christians hiding out in their houses, turning off the lights. All the kids in the neighborhood know that you are the weird Christian family, afraid of masks and candy.

What I do is I make sure every kid that comes to my door gets *more candy* than any other house because as Christians, we are blessed to be blessing. With that candy, they get a non-judgmental tract talking about salvation. While that kid is eating that candy, his little heart is open for information and while he fingers through that tract, a seed is planted in his heart that one day brings him to the family. I have taken Satan's day away from him. Rule-worshiping Christians are missing the greatest evangelizing day ever. What other day do you have kids coming to your house where you can give them a tract?

Understand; my kids are not allowed to dress up as evil, and we explain why. But what is wrong with them dressing up and getting candy? We give no glory to Satan in it, so what is wrong with it? We talk to them about how awesome it is to give to the neighborhood. They take part in all that. See, I don't have the weird kid at school that has to leave the room during the Halloween party, alienating him and making school and his social life harder than it has to be.

There is big portion of my generation with a hardened conscience. Go online and type "Smurfs are evil" or type "Care Bears are evil" and you will find a list of millions of people who have written articles on how they left the church because there was a group of religious people who walled their kids off. To this day, I don't know how you get the idea that Care Bears are evil. The Love Care Bear is evil, how? The Peace Bear and Joy Bear are evil, how?

All these rules in the church and kids locked up by parents who wouldn't let them do anything. When they turned eighteen-years-old, they jumped into the world because those rules made no sense. There was no *why* to the madness. Their consciences became hardened because they were sick of feeling guilt and suffering condemnation.

So, they said, "I might as well party. I'm going to hell anyway. I might as well have fun around here."

My mom once came home from a church service and said, "You can't watch the Smurfs. They're evil."

Jason and I loved the Smurfs, so we said, "Mom, watch one episode of the Smurfs with us."

She sat down, and we watched. The Smurfs did good, brought joy, and overcame the evil. She said, "Yeah, you can watch that. I don't see anything evil or wrong with that." Kudos to Mom!

Parents, just because someone says something is evil, that doesn't make it evil. Make sure you check it out. Read the book. Watch the show. Obviously, I don't have to watch *Texas Chain Saw Massacre* to know it is inappropriate for my six-year-old. But for certain things that you aren't sure, *become sure*.

Some parents say, "We don't let our boys play with toy guns." Why? Go read James Dobson's *Raising Up Boys*. It is an important part of their development. I grew up playing cops and robbers, cowboys, and I am a great person. I never once had the desire to go and really kill someone. Play guns and real guns are very different. I don't have time to explain. Go read the book.

So, it is important to listen to our children a little bit and then do some investigation. Just because the TBN pastor says something is evil does not make it evil. Dig in and find out. Make sure that your kids feel like you are doing what is fair. We want to protect their hearts, but we want to make sure that it's not leading them into silliness or legalism.

It does something for your kids when they know you really do your homework. "Son, I don't know if this book is good or not. We are going to look through it and let you know." Once you look through it, you can then say, "It is fine," or, "No, it is not. Let me tell you why."

"Harry Potter is evil." Really? Why? "Well, Pastor, because they do magic and kids that watch it will turn to Wicca." Does that *really* make sense to you? Even if they did turn to Wicca, they wouldn't stay long. They would find out that you can't fly on a broom. You can't use a wand to change things. You can't drink a potion and make a man. We are talking fairy tale. Kids at the age of four can tell you the difference.

Things to Do
Let's finish this chapter on the things to do (and not do) with your child's conscience.

Number 1: I will always love you.
Don't manipulate children with the loss of your love. Some parents say, "If you do this, I'll love you," or "You were bad. Mom doesn't love you right now."

I love my children because they exist. I will love them unconditionally for the rest of their lives. I don't care what they do. "I still love you." They can make the biggest mistake possible. "I love you like God loves you. I love you unconditionally. There are no conditions on my love. I don't like the sin, but I love you." Your children need to be secure in your love. You are the picture of Father God. "Sin I hate. You I love. You don't have to earn my love. You always have it."

Number 2: Guilt left too long is no good.
Don't make your child feel guilty for long periods of time. God is a God of forgiveness, and He forgets. We will really get into this when we get to discipline later in the book, but for now, a little guilt is good. Then, we forgive, and we pull them out of that guilty feeling. We go right back to restoring the relationship and showing them that you love them.

Guilt left inside for too long turns into anger, which turns into hate. Hate hardens the conscience, which prevents them from making good choices.

Questions for Review:

1. What is contained in the Wisdom Warehouse?

2. What are the conscience's responsibilities?

3.   How does the conscience try to get you to do what it believes is right?

4.   What does understanding do?

5.   What are the three types of why's and what should your response be for each of them?

Your Scenario for Discussion:

Your three-year-old throws a major tantrum at the grocery store. What do you do?

This Week at Home:

Married Couples: Dads, make sure you are doing couch time as described in *More Than a Dad*. Make sure every night Mom gets the first fifteen minutes of your night. Then spend time with the kids. Also make sure you plan a date with Mom. Describe to the group what effect this had on the children.

Everyone: Be prepared to share with the class some examples of using why with your kids, and what the outcome was.

Homework for Dad and Mom:

Read Chapter 4 and 5 of *More Than a Dad/More than a Mom*.

CHAPTER 4:
Self-Control

The Jar of Character

Before we get to self-control, the second of the virtues to instill in your children, I want to encourage you to do the following: create a *Jar of Character*. This activity is very effective for ages four and up, but you can probably start as early as three. The child gets a jar with his or her name on it. The child starts with five marbles inside. The jar is all about exceeding expectations. Whenever the child goes beyond my Biblical expectations, they get a marble. Whenever the child's actions are below my expectations, they lose a marble. If expectations are met, nothing happens.

I expect that my kids will be nice to each other and talk respectfully to one another. That is what I expect. If one of my children gives up his favorite toy for the other child (without me prompting them), that goes beyond my expectations. He will receive a marble.

I expect that my kids get up in the morning, get ready for school and do their chores. They do not get a marble for doing what is expected. If they go to school, and I noticed that the kitchen is not done, they lose a marble. If they go overboard and decide to do extra cleaning, they get a marble. If the chores are done but not done 100%, they lose a marble. If the chores are done perfectly, that is what is expected.

Understand that this is age sensitive. My expectations are different for my seven-year-old and for my 12-year-old. My four-year-old made his bed on his own. It looked horrible, but he was so proud of the extra work he did. I gave him a marble. For this time in his life, his action was beyond my expectations.

Suppose that we are entering a restaurant, and my seven-year-old gets up ahead and holds the door for Mom. That was beyond my expectations; a marble will be given. In time, this action will become my expectation for him. My fourteen-year-old does the same, no marble (door-holding is expected at this age).

If one of my kids says something mean to the other, that is below my expectations; please go get me a marble.

For Those Who Are New to the Program
Your expectations might start out lower initially. Let me explain why. Suppose that your kids have never done first-time obedience. For this week, every time they do first-time obedience, doing so exceeds your expectations (for one week only; maybe two.) Next week, first-time obedience becomes the expectation.

So, each week you will explain the new virtues you introduce and give your child some basic why's. When the virtue is demonstrated, a marble goes in the jar. (To me, giving the marbles is the strongest teaching tool. It keeps your children looking to do good, and it keeps you looking for and rewarding good behavior. They may even get really excited to remind you, "Look, Mom, I did what you asked!")

When they fail to perform this week's virtue, you remind them that next week they will lose a marble for that failure to act.

They do lose marbles for actions from previous weeks. So, if first-time obedience was introduced two weeks ago, and you ask them to do something, and they don't do it, you ask them to remove a number of marbles (based on the seriousness). If they throw a fit about it, you ask them to remove more. If it continues, they get sent to their room, and we deal with that as rebellion. (You will find out how in Chapter 10.)

When we get to discipline, we will cover how to guide them through a lot of these situations. It is important that you don't start any new discipline routines at this time. Discipline done right will raise kids of great character, but discipline done wrong will actually do more damage than no discipline at all. I encourage you to wait until we have gone through and taught discipline before you start any new discipline adventures.

At the end of the week, if they have a certain number of marbles, then there is a reward (extra video game time, ice cream, Peter Piper Pizza. Something within reason). If the marbles aren't there, then there is a consequence (no TV, extra chores. Again, whatever is reasonable).

If my kids run out of marbles, or lose too many in a day, or at the end of the week haven't gained enough, I look at the context of the week, and then we move onto consequences in their lives.

What We Love About This
All parents have a discipline line. Cross it, and you're in trouble. Kids know the line, where the line is, and how to get right up to it, but not cross it. They stay below the radar, just mean enough to their brother to keep you just scolding them day after day, nothing more. Just selfish enough to keep you from discipline. Whining just enough to keep you locked into that *day-after-frustrating day* we talked about earlier.

With the Character Jar, those little actions add up, but even for something small, there is more of a consequence than me scolding you. "That was rude to your brother. Go take a marble out of the jar. Now come back and tell me why that was wrong." (It is so powerful when we have them dig into their own warehouse and tell you why.) That right there may be enough to keep them from teasing their younger brother. Scolding them day after day hasn't changed a thing. Losing a marble might help them remember to make their bed, unlike a daily scolding that has never worked.

The Character Jar teaches them that there are natural rewards in life for going beyond the expected, and consequences for going below what is expected.

What makes perfect is that there is no reward for doing what is expected, which reiterates that our kids should do good out of the love for goodness, not for the reward.

That is why you never get to a store and say, "If you behave in the store, I will get you some candy." No, what is expected is that you behave. The child is not Shamu who gets a fish for doing a trick.

Now, when we get to the check-out line, I may say, "Kids, I am so proud of how you behaved. Pick out some candy." They were good because that is how we act, not to get something.

Just Say, "No" to Rebellion
Acts of rebellion, as we discuss later, have nothing to do with the jar. If I tell you to do something and you say, "No," losing a marble isn't the solution. Flat out rebellion is very serious, and we will treat it as such (but not until Chapter 10).

Right now, with your eight-year-old, you go through the same problems day after day. That's because what they do is never enough for a big consequence. Instead, Mom and Dad yell at them. "How many times do I have to tell you to stop being mean to your brother? How come you haven't done your chores?" (They did them for the last three days in a row but today, they forgot, so punishment is just a tongue lashing.) Now there is a simple and easy way for you.

"Laken, go take a marble out of your jar."
"Why, Dad?"
"You tell me," I say.
He looks around and says, "I forgot to do the dishes."
"Yep."

That's not a casual example. So many great things happened. Let's go through them. One, there was a consequence. Two, Laken had to discover and acknowledge what he didn't do. If, instead, I continue to tell him what he did wrong, he never has to remember. He never learns responsibility.

Teaching Your Kid Responsibility:
Your child is going to school. Mom says, "Did you brush your teeth? Make your bed? Take a shower? Do your chores? Do you have your homework? Do you have on clean underwear and clean socks? Turn off your light?" The child has no reason to remember anything. You will do it all for him. And you live day after day frustrated because your kids can't ever remember anything. You are not building a responsible adult.

Instead, the simple question should be, "Are you ready for school?" That covers it all. Now, they have to ask, did I brush my teeth, did I make my bed, is my homework in my backpack? You no longer take responsivities away from the child; the child is learning to be responsible. Forget something? They face the consequence. You have helped them become ready to be a successful, responsible adult.

"Mom, can I go out and play?"

You used to say, "Did you do your homework, finish the dishes, pick up your toys?" Now you say, "Can you?" They go through their internal list. 'Oops, I have to go pick up my toys first." It becomes *their* responsibility.

Virtue 2: Self-Control

Wisdom and understanding mean nothing if our children do not learn self-control. It doesn't matter that the warehouse is full, because when the conscience tells them what they should do, they lack the self-control to do what is right.

Self-control is the ability to govern oneself. It's the ability to make the tough right choice rather than the fun wrong choice. It's the ability to do what *is* right, not what *feels* right. It means teaching our children not to do what they want right now, but instead, to do what is needed. None of the character traits taught will be worth anything if your child does not have the self-control to make the right choices in life and follow through.

Self-control actually could be called success control. Your self-control will determine the success you have in life. Without it, you will destroy your life. We, as parents, will train our children to control themselves.

Self-control enables our children to control their tempers, control their sensual appetites (helping them abstain from premarital bad choices, and affairs when they are married) and resist temptations (remember that weed?) It enables them to wait and to delay gratification in the service of higher and distant goals. They will rule their desires and emotions, because if they don't, then their desires and emotions will rule them.

All the wisdom and understanding in the world will do a person no good if he or she doesn't have the self-control to apply them to his or her life. In our children, we need to instill a habit of self-control in their lives.

Self-control is like a muscle. The more we use it, the stronger it becomes. Many Christians fall into horrible circumstances because that muscle is so weak.

When you first learn to stand up as a child, it takes a lot of work— a tremendous amount of energy and determination. But as you work those muscles, it gets easier and easier, until one day, you don't even have to think about it. You just stand up. Even though your body got bigger, the task seemed to get easier. It's the same with self- control. In the early years, it is hard for the kids, but as they use that muscle over and over, and though the temptations of life get bigger, without even thinking about it, they are controlling themselves.

What Does the Self Actually Need to Control?
Self-control is teaching your children to control their thoughts. This is vital because your thoughts control every part of your life. The Bible says, "As a man thinks so is he." As your child thinks like a person of great character, so is he. As your child thinks responsibly, so is he.

Your child's thoughts control his actions and control his emotions. The Bible says *capture your thoughts*. Think on the good, holy, pure, and noteworthy. Think only on these things. If your child can think on happy thoughts, good things, then depression has no place in his life. If your child thinks anger and getting even, then he or she loses control, and does things outside of Godly character. In this chapter, we will focus on the heart—on the thoughts. If we can get them to control themselves from the inside, the outside will naturally follow.

The Transition of Control
Teaching your children self-control is a process of you first controlling them on the outside, then transitioning them to controlling themselves from the inside. You have to be their self-control until they are able to control themselves. In the younger years, you use your authority to control them. In the teenage years, you use the strength of your relational influence to help them control themselves. But know this—if you cannot control your four-year-old, do not think for one minute your fifteen-year-old will have any self-control.

Teach Your Kids to Fly
Teaching self-control is similar to teaching someone to fly an airplane. The airplane is your child's life. The goal is not to crash the life. You first start out with them in the passenger seat while you fly the plane. You make sure the plane doesn't get into danger,

turning it this way and that. You are in full control of the plane, where it goes, what it does. What it eats, when it eats, when it sleeps, where it plays . . . age zero to around four.

The next stage is your children at the controls while you sit beside them. At any given time, you may grab hold of the controls to keep them out of danger, but you are teaching them how to fly their own lives. You give them instructions on what to do, how to do it, and why it is being done. If they don't listen, then you have to grab the wheel from them. You may tell them not to hang out with a friend, for example, but sometimes you have to *make sure* they don't hang out with that friend. This is for children aged four to teens.

There then comes the time (around junior high) when you aren't right beside them anymore. They are around friends, making choices all day long and you won't be there. You are on the ground while they are flying the plane. You are talking to them, instructing them on what they need to do so they don't crash. But really, they are in control.

Many teenagers have crashed their lives because Mom and Dad did not transition properly, teach properly, and the kids refused to listen. When I'm on the ground and they are flying, it is Mom's and Dad's relationship, the trust they put into the hearts of their kids, the character instilled, and the self-control learned that will determine whether or not they will listen to you. (In Chapter 10, you will learn that at this age, I sometimes do have to ground the plane.)

Sorry, No Flying Today
Age doesn't mean the automatically get to fly. You are in control until they can control themselves. They don't get the airplane until you know they will be responsible with it. If your two-year-old can't be in a restaurant without screaming and ruining everyone else's time, you must have the character to take the child home. If your child can't hang out with a friend without getting into trouble,

then that friend is removed from his life. You have to make choices for the child until the child can make right choices.

The thing you must understand is this; just because a child can't handle a situation and make right choices does not mean he is a bad kid. Kids mature at different rates. One of your kids might be able to choose his own friends at an early age. He just seems to get it. Another child raised in the same home may not be picking good friends in high school. That aspect is just an area of immaturity.

In such a case, your stance is, "You are more important to me than anything. Until you can pick right friends, I will pick them for you. Until you can make right choices, I have to choose for you."

They may not be able to fly by themselves at a certain age. If the child says, "I'm sixteen. I can pick my own friends," my response is, "Obviously, you can't pick your own friends. Until you can make right choices, I will make your choices for you. I did not spend sixteen years of my life pouring into you to allow a few friends to destroy your future. If I have to, I will go to school with you, sit with you; eat with you. I will do whatever it takes to make sure you don't make a life-destroying decision. Until you can pick right friends, I am your only friend." We will discuss laying down your life for your kids later.

Many parents ask, "When can my daughter start dating?" How would I know? Every girl is different. If your seventeen-year-old daughter is dating a twenty-seven-year-old loser, getting herself into bad situations, then she is obviously not mature enough to date. And as a parent, you have to make her choices until she can make the right ones.

You might say, "Well, she will just sneak out."

The answer is, "Not in my house. I will have an alarm on the house. I will take off from work and go to school with you, I will be by your side twenty-four hours a day if I have to, because I will not allow you to ruin your life." She may hate you now, but one day she will thank you for loving her enough to lay down your life for her and for her future.

In this process, you are constantly giving them new responsibilities in their lives. At each stage, the responsibilities get larger and larger. One day, around age four to five, you might tell your son or daughter, "When you get up, you make your bed." (They should have been helping you for the last couple of years.) In time, you'll add, "take a shower, comb your hair, make some cereal."

One day, at age seven, they are up ready for school all on their own. At a young age, they have learned the self-control it takes to be responsible every morning. You apply this to all areas of life. You should not have to remind your third grader to do their homework, practice the piano, or do their chores. They know what to do. Now let's teach them how to work out that self-control muscle on their own.

Like Anything Else, It Starts with You!
Self-control, like any virtue, starts with you. They will learn from your example, not your words. If you don't have control, neither will they. If you lack self-control, today is the time to start exercising it. *Work that thing out all day long.* Get all the books and tapes you need to fix that problem in your life. If you can't do it for you, do it for them.

Is Good, Not Feels Good
As we move to the next section, we really want you to see how each of these steps are teaching your children a central lesson: we don't do what feels good. We do what is good. We do what is best for you, not what you want to do. From the time they born, we are moving them out of Level 1 character and getting them closer to do what will produce their best life.

Life is about giving up what I want, for what I want most. I may want candy all day, but I want to be healthy more. I may want to say mean things, but I want great relationships more. Teaching our kids this sets them up for living a life that attains what they want most.

When Do I Start Teaching Self-Control?
Self-control needs to be taught when the child is born. Yes, at that initial stage, you already begin parenting today for what you want tomorrow. You do not pick up your child every time the child cries. If your child has been fed, changed, played with, and loved on, the child is fine. It actually is healthy for the child to cry. It develops their lungs.

If you pick the child up every time they cry and hold them all the time, you are setting up your future with the baby to be near impossible. You are also making it very hard for anyone who has to watch the child.

The child is very smart. "I cry. Mom picks me up. I want to be held all the time." (The child doesn't need to be held all the time. It is that Level 1 of character, doing what feels good, not what is good.) "I cry whenever I do not get my way."

Listen, KIDS DO WHAT WORKS! BABIES DO WHAT WORKS! If crying gets them what they want, they will do that. If crying does not work, they'll stop crying. A child that is held all the time turns into a toddler that throws fits. Parent today for tomorrow.

If you do not pick up the crying baby, they learn very quickly that crying gets them nothing. So why do it? Put your child on a feeding schedule, once again teaching self-control. Children that are fed whenever they want, (called *demand feeding*, or stealing-all-of-Mom's-time-and-joy feeding) are very unhappy, and the parents are confused. "Is the cry for food? Is it for affection? Is it for who knows what? Fine, have a bottle." Demand feeding a baby is setting you up for a very hard time with the child. A feeding schedule is a better choice.

Ask your doctor, but most say put the newborn on a three-hour feeding schedule. What is also amazing about this is your child will be sleeping through the night in six weeks. This is what is done in the hospital. Why change when you get home?

If the baby has been fed, played with and changed and is screaming, put the child in bed or in the playpen, close the door, and do what you need to do until the next feeding. In just a week, that child is a happy baby, able to control himself most of the time. The child may cry right when you put him down, but a few moments later, the child is happy and playing or sleeping. At three-weeks-old, you have already started teaching self-control.

Stop Being Mean to the Baby. Don't Give Them Bad Habits.
Your baby should never ever sleep with you. In the beginning, the baby may sleep better, *but you won't*. Your rest is crucial to being a great parent. At an early age, you have put a habit in the child of still sleeping in your bed. Why do parents put habits into their child that the child then has to suffer to break?

Now, sleeping with the parents is an emotional deal at age one, two, or five to break, but we parent today for tomorrow. The child gets into a habit of sleeping in his own bed. If the child is fed at night and is crying, close the door, turn off the baby monitor, set your alarm for the next feeding time. In no time, the baby has learned self-control.

For example, parents think it is so cute for the child to need their blanky. "Where's your blanky? Can't go anywhere without it!" Then, one day, when the child is throwing a fit because you can't find it, you say, "It's time you were done with it." They wouldn't need to be done with it if you didn't force the habit on them.

Have you have been frustrated for years, looking for the stupid thing? You forced the habit on them. Around three months old, we got rid of the blanky. My kids don't need it. Stop giving them habits they are going to have to break. (It is interesting that none of my children ever sucked their thumb. I think that the overuse of the binky could attribute to this bad habit.)

Your children can go to sleep at three months old without their special blanket, without their binky, their stupid bear. Stop being cruel. How would you like it if someone forced cocaine in you every night, and then, once you got hooked, made you quit? That's mean. A child doesn't need a special cup, a special bowl, or a special blanket. All you are doing is making your job tomorrow harder.

I say, make parenting as easy as you can. When I go to leave, I don't have to worry about a special blanket or special cup. I just go. And it is so weird. My kids don't have habits at age four that need to be broken.

The Playpen, My Best Friend
So many moms can't be a great mom because they have no time in their lives. This is how you find time and teach your baby self-control.

Your baby needs to learn playpen time. This exercise in self-control teaches your child to learn boundaries. The child plays in a confined area. It teaches the child to focus. You give the child one or two toys and for thirty minutes to an hour, they play.

ADHD spreads because parents are not teaching children boundaries or self- control. We let our babies roam all over the house and get into whatever they want. They can play anywhere in the house. They're never taught to sit and focus on one thing. Focus is a skill that is learned, not something God puts into some kids and not into others. Focus is actually self-control.

Suppose your kids are taught to do whatever they want and go wherever they want for their first five years. Then, they're taken to school and told to sit in this chair and don't move for two hours.

Why can't they? It must be a chemical imbalance, so we shoot them full of drugs to numb them to life. The child suffers because the parents never taught the child or trained the child to focus and to have self-control.

Around age two, transition your children from playpen time to room time. They play in their room, with just a few toys for thirty to sixty minutes. Maybe they draw or color or whatever. (They do have the self-control not to color on the walls and tables.) It is important that this happens every day. I was impressed that Laken and Camille (my son and daughter-in-law) were told by their family physician to do just that. The doctor was emphatic, adding that it's important to limit the screen time a child gets to an hour a day. The doctor said children's television shows are made to switch scenes every three to six seconds. Though it looks like the kid is focusing, passive viewing works against the child.

You Play Here!
We're going to emphasize that the children don't get to play anywhere they want in the house. Self-control is taught as soon as the child becomes mobile. "These rooms are not for you. You may play in here and there, though." Children are taught they don't get into the cupboards. They don't play with outlets. As soon as the child becomes mobile, you teach self-control.

Children don't turn on the TV. They don't play with adult things. That's why they have toys. Mommy's keys are not toys. The remote is not a toy. You do not baby-proof your house; you house-proof your baby. This way you can go to other people's houses, and they don't have to put all the breakables up. You have put self-control into your six-month-old child.

Naptime Designed by God
There is another way Mom finds time to do what she needs to do, but it also is very, very healthy and important for your children. Babies and toddlers need a nap.

For children, all the way up until they go to school, there is nap time. From zero to three, they get two (yes *two*) two-hour naps a day. A fourteen-month-old goes down, cries for a bit, goes to sleep, and then you, not the child, decide when the nap is up.

After two hours, if baby is up playing in the crib, I get him up. Baby does not start crying, and I come and get him. You wake up happy, and when you are happy, I will get you.

It's the same thing in the morning. Parents are up at five every morning. Why? "Well, that is when our two-year-old gets up." That is the difference between your stressed-out life and mine. My two-year-old gets up when I get up. My two-year-old gets up happy. On Saturday, my two-year-old gets up around eight o'clock. My two-year-old has self-control.

Bedtime is When I Say
It is very important that your children have a reasonable bedtime. That brings structure into their lives. By the time they are in junior high, they know how to go to bed at a right time so they can be successful in life. It's self-control.

Do our kids fall asleep on their own watching TV? No, no, they need to learn at a very young age to sleep without any sleep aids. Many adults struggle going to sleep because parents put wrong habits in them.

Children up to the age of five should be in bed by 8-8:30. Kids should not be up past 8:30 until they are in junior high. (On weekends of course, they can stay up a little longer.)

Scheduling is very important. For one thing, it is consistent. Kids want to know what is expected. They know that this is the bedtime. Two, it is great for Mom and Dad. You now have time to spend with each other, and to get other things done. You can unwind and get ready for tomorrow.

If the kids get up when you get up, and then go to sleep when you go to sleep, this is very hard on the marriage, and very hard on you. (If you are single, it is equally good to unwind and get things in order.) Doctors second this recommendation. It is a lot healthier for them.

I'm afraid! Don't Be!
All kids will be afraid. Going to bed is when you will usually encounter this fear. Many parents actually encourage the fear without knowing they are doing so. They turn on the light and/or stay with the child until they go to sleep.

It is very important that you put the self-control in them that allows no fear. You don't want to be cruel, but you slowly train them not to allow that fear to grab hold of them.

We never allow our kids to sleep with the lights on, but we will leave a hall light on, and a closet light. We will never sleep with them or stay with them until they go to sleep (unless they are sick).

When they say they are scared we say, "Don't be." That always gets a funny look from them. "But Mom, I'm scared."

"Don't be!" Mom replies. Then we explain that there's nothing to be scared about, and Mom and Dad are right out there. "We would never allow anything to happen to you."

"But mom, I'm really scared!"

We reply again, "Don't be, we love you. Good night." This process teaches our kids to control their thoughts. Not to allow the fear to rule their lives. They have self-control being worked out inside them at a really young age.

When they are adults, and some circumstances in life look a little dark, they can trust that God is right there. He would never let anything happen to them. They respond to life out of faith, not out of fear. We raise adults who tell themselves "Don't Be Afraid!"

Food Fight? I Say, "No!"
Your baby needs to learn that we don't play with our food. We don't put food in our hair. We don't throw food. Teach that as soon as you start feeding them baby food. Right away, I take their hand away from the food. I teach them how to control themselves during meals. You don't get to put your hands into the food. Until I say you are old enough, you don't get to hold the spoon; I do. Teach this right away. Then, it isn't that hard to teach your eight-month- old how to eat food the correct way. Parent today for what you want tomorrow.

Baby does not decide what he will eat. We do. Baby does not just get fruits. Baby does not always get what he wants. The child gets what he needs. "Well, our baby won't eat vegetables." In my house, I guarantee he would. By giving the child what he needs, you are already starting the process of moving out of Level 1 character. Baby always gets veggies first, fruits last. Your child then grows up not being a picky eater. Picky eaters are created, not born (an Anderson theory; not a proven fact).

I Want the Blue, No Red, No Green, No … Cup!
Children definitely do not always get to choose. "I'm sorry, little Johnny, toast and eggs are for breakfast. You definitely don't get to choose the color of the bowl or cup." Parents get themselves into this choosing war. The reason is that children are too young to handle the responsibility of choice. My kids are happy with whatever color cup they get. Drinking milk isn't a debate. If you don't give them the option, then you take away that frustrating experience of choice. (We will talk more in later chapters about kids being addicted to choice and how to transition them to where they are responsible enough to handle choices.)

Teach Control of Emotions

Children should learn right away to control emotions. I do not give into fits at three-weeks-old, nor do I at any older age. Many parents are so frustrated at the store and in public because the child is throwing a fit, but that is probably what is allowed at home. You parent at home for how they will act in public. If fits get them their way at home, don't be surprised at the store. An emotional fit or complete loss of self-control should *never* be rewarded! When there is no reward, there is no reason for the fit—too much work for no reward.

How Do I Handle a Fit?
A fit is easy in my house. Baby goes right into crib. Toddler is told, "Go sit on the bed until you are done. You may get off your bed when you are finished." We are teaching our kids at a very young age to control their emotions. This is a facet of self-control.

We were watching my two-year-old granddaughter one night. She got fired up and started crying (this is rare, she is very good). I was proud that my kids had already been doing this with her. I said, "Go to your room you can come out when you're done."

She screamed "I'm done, I'm done."

"No, not till you done crying." I guided her to her room. She escalated, got louder. I reminded her we don't get loud. If you're loud, I will close the door. As I started closing the door, she got quieter. I reiterated that she could come our when she was done. About thirty seconds later, she gathered herself, and said "I'm done."

I smiled and said, "Okay, come on out." This works, even for grandpa.

Now, if the fit escalates to rebellion where they are all out throwing stuff in the room, stomping, screaming, then we move to the discipline area (which will come later). They moved past emotions and into rebellion, trying to blackmail you into giving them what they want. That doesn't happen in my house. I tell my toddler, "You can throw a fit, but make it quiet." Each of my children escalated a fit a couple of times, but never again. We will get to that.

Aha! Got You Mom and Dad
Fits in public are a little harder. Most of the time, if we take care of it at home, it doesn't come up in public. If you are consistent at home, fits in public are rare. Remember we parent at home for what we want in public.

But for a fit in public, I whisper in a stern voice, "Stop." Because you respect other people, and they shouldn't have to listen to your child, you may have to leave the store. You must NEVER ever give in to the fit. If you give in once, next time it will be worse. Break the habit now, so tomorrow is easier.

Get Happy or I'll Make You Happy
Older kids are not allowed a fit any more than younger ones. If I say, "Clean your room. You are not allowed to storm through the house, talking under your breath, slamming doors. You say, 'Yes, Mom. Yes, Dad,' and force a smile if you have to. Go and do what I ask. Anything less is unacceptable."

Sure, a lot of times they force the happiness, but the interesting thing about life is when you make yourself act happy, you become happy. It's not long after they force the smile that they are laughing doing the dishes.

This is a must! Your children need to have the self-control to do what you ask with a happy heart. I am parenting today to help my kids tomorrow. There will be a time in their life when their boss will ask them to do a job they don't want to. Successful people put a smile on and do their best. Their spouse one day will ask them to do something they don't want to (maybe every day). Our kids put a smile on and show love towards their spouse. A happy life is having the self-control to be happy in all circumstances.

First-Time Obedience
Your children must always do what you ask the first time you ask it. It's first-time obedience. That is the standard. Your children must learn at an early age to obey when asked and do it with a happy heart. Anything less undermines everything else you do in this series. This is one of the greatest ways to work out that self-control muscle. What makes this so amazing is that as they get older, it is just a habit. "Yes, Mom," comes so easy.

How Many Times Do I Have to Call You? Oh Yeah, Just Once.
When you call your kids, they come and say, "Yes, Mom?" or, 'Yes, Dad?" They don't scream across the house, "What?" Exercise self-control.

Yeah, Whatever Mom!
100% of the time, your kids must talk to both parents with a respectful tone and respectful words. I don't care how old are. They don't lose marbles for this. We move right to discipline. It is unacceptable to be mouthy, sassy, or use an angry tone with Mom or Dad, but especially with Mom. If you don't get the self-control in the younger years, Mom is going to have a heck of a time with the teenager telling her where to go and to blankety-blank off. Don't even mess around with this one. (If not, we go right to Chapter 10.) This includes heavy sighs, rolling eyes, or that evil glare.

"No, you will for the rest of your life, honor your parents." It is so important because this is the only commandment that has a promise of a long life.

I Doooon't Waaaant Toooooo!
Whining is a form of rebellion. If left alone, it can cause both you and your children years of frustration. Whining is a weenie tantrum. It is interesting to see how many parents reward whining but feel that the reprimand with the reward is going to solve it. Yet

it never does. And your two-year-old whiner one day has become this fifteen-year-old unhappy, whinny adult.

For example, suppose the child comes up to you and in a whiney tone says, "I need a drink!"

You respond sternly, "That is not how we ask! What do you say?"

The child, still in a whinny voice, says, "Pleeeeese, can I have a drink?"

You say, "Okay, but no more whining."

Don't be surprised the next time the child asks for a drink in that same whinny tone. THERE IS NO REASON FOR THE CHILD TO CHANGE BEHAVIORs.

The child got exactly what the child wanted.

Instead, say, "Mommy is going to set the kitchen timer for one minute. When it goes off, you may come back and ask me correctly." Once again, you didn't coach the child on exactly what to say. The child has to go and come back on his own with the proper phrase. You can never give in to whining. My children know that whining will never get them what they want.

Control Those Things
To be self-controlled, your children need to learn to control their emotions. The Bible says every evil comes out of uncontrolled emotions. We teach our children that our emotions do not control us. We control our emotions. We tell them where to go and they take us there. You have kids on Prozac for depression. That child doesn't need drugs. The child needs self-control. Unhappiness is not an option in the Anderson home. You put a smile on your face.

You come down to breakfast happy or go back upstairs until you are. We do things with a joyful heart. My Bible says rejoice in the

Lord ALWAYS. Anything else is below the standard. Once again, your children follow your example. It is time parents got happy. You can force a smile and a kind word for the co-worker. Why is it you can't give your family at least the same consideration? The co-worker is out of your life in a few years. Kids will be influenced for a lifetime.

"Pastor, you don't understand. I'm unhappy." Well, force a smile on when around your kids. Act happy just like we tell our kids to do. And in the comfort of your room, you can be as miserable as you want. If you can't act happy for yourself, at least do it for the kids. Funny thing is, if you act happy long enough, you actually become happy.

The Basics
Basic courtesies are self-control. Don't litter. Open the door for people. Say please and thank you. All are part of self-control that we need to be instilling in their hearts.

Between six and seven, children should be getting ready for school, making the bed and doing chores on their own—all self-control. They should be able to do well in school, but more importantly, have the self-control to get good marks in character. I am more concerned about these than I am with an "A" in math.

Can You Please Shut That Kid Up?
Have you ever been in a restaurant and suffer the child who has no inside voice? "MOM, MOM, MOM. I WANT THE CHICKEN AND FRENCH FRIES!!!!!! MOM, I GOT TO GO PEE!!!"

This family puts me over the edge. They interrupt all of our enjoyable times because their child has no self-control. I don't care if your child is twelve months old—they are taught to love and respect other people. When in public, we respect and love others enough not to ruin their time. *If my child can't do that, then I can't go out in public.*

At home, you teach your kids the *inside voice*. You are teaching them not only self-control, but how to be considerate and love others.

One lady's child screamed inside a restaurant for ever and ever. She overheard someone make a comment. Her loud response was, "We have just as much a right to be here as anyone else." That statement lacks character. Can I have a loud party at my house that keeps you up all night? It is my house. I have rights, right? No, character says that my rights can never infringe on your rights. I have a right to enjoy my meal just like you do. But I do not have the right to be loud and take away your rights.

Being parents of character, we teach our children how to act in public and how to love others by respecting them. This training, of course, starts at home. It can't be said enough: train at home how you want them to act in public.

What! What! What!
Have you ever been conversing with someone and their child interrupts? "Mom, Mom, Mom, Mom!" That shows a lack of self-control. Teach your children the *interrupt rule*. The child puts her hand on your side or leg, letting you know she has something to tell you. You put your hand on her hand, letting her know that when you get a break in the conversation, you will find out what she needs. Then, tell the other person, "Hold on. My daughter has a question."

You can begin doing this with your kids as early as they can talk. Start this as soon as possible. (This week, make a game out of it with your kids.) The children learn that they are not the center of the universe, and they need to be respectful to other people. It is about controlling themselves.

Just Say, "Hi!"

Someone says, "Hi," to your child. Your child responds minimally with a "Hi" back. Even if shy, they have enough self-control to make themselves give a common courtesy.

I am sure there are many more self-control issues you can be working on in your home. Can you think of some of your own?

Questions for Review:

1. What does self-control actually control?

2. Have you seen any area of self-control in your life in that is lacking and that one of your kids struggle with that same area? If so, what are you doing to change that?

3. List out some areas of self-control you will be changing this week in your home.

Your Scenario for Discussion:

Your fourteen-year-old is caught hanging out with friends you specifically asked them not to be around.

This Week at Home:

- Be prepared to share your experience with the Jar of Character. What changes did you see with your kids? Make it a game!
- Sit the kids down and let them know what areas of self-control on which you are working. Make it fun. "Okay,

Mom is going to call you. You are to come and say, "Yes, Mom?" When I ask you do to something, you are going to do it." Do this a couple of times right there.
- When your kids don't practice the self-control, let them know how that behavior was unacceptable, and when we get to Chapter 10, there are going to be consequences. This is only fair to your kids that you give them some time to get out of their old habits. Give them a few weeks of learning the new expectations of the home. This is the game.
- Explain to the group what happened this week with the game.

Homework for Mom and Dad:

Read Chapters 6 and 7 from *More Than a Dad/More than a Mom* books.

CHAPTER 5:
Love

Selfless love that expects nothing back is the most powerful force in the universe. Its impact on both the giver and the receiver is incalculable.
~Washington Jarvis

Virtue 3: Love

They asked Jesus to sum up the Bible by asking the most important thing we can do. He said *love*. Love God, love others, love yourself. Learning how to love is the most important thing in life. It is what life is all about. We were created to love and to walk in love. You will never experience life in the way you should until you do what you were created to do. Until you learn how to walk in love, you will not experience peace, joy, happiness, and a sense of fulfillment to the level your creator intended. The greatest moments of your life will always be tied to love.

I Corinthians 13:1-3 talks about how you can do so many great things in life, but if you don't have love, you have nothing. You can gain the whole world, but without love, and someone to share it with, what does it matter? We as parents can raise our kids to be successful in so many areas, but if we do not teach them love, it will not matter.

One of the most important things you will do as a parent is getting love into that warehouse of your children. Getting them to a place where they understand love—the importance of it. You teach them what real love is.

They need to know that Hollywood and God have a different idea of what love is. Hollywood tries to teach us that love is a feeling, it is here today, maybe gone tomorrow. You might find your sleeping beauty, but in a few years, she might fall out of love with you and run off with the new dwarf "horny." That kind of love brings pain, hurt, and break up.

The world's love is selfish. How I feel, how I fell out of love, and how my needs aren't being met.

God's Love Is So Much Different

I Corinthians 13:4-8 says love suffers long and is kind, love does not envy, love does not parade itself, is not puffed up. Does not behave rudely, does not seek its own, is not provoked, thinks no evil. Does not rejoice in iniquity, but rejoices in the truth, bears all things believes all things, hopes all things, endures all thing.

The world's love almost always fails. God's kind of love never fails.

God's love is not about what I *get*; it is about what I *give*. Real love is not about me. It's about you. I can't fall out of it—I can only quit doing it. What do I mean by "quit"?

God's kind of love is a verb, or an action. It is something you do. The fruit, or the result of doing it, is the feeling we call love. If you want the feeling, then you have to do the action. If you don't feel love for your wife, it means you have stopped loving her.

But starting today, if you became concerned with her needs and started loving her, buying flowers for her, taking her out, thinking about her, doing for her, in no time you would feel love for her.

Look Beyond the Reasons

"But Pastor, you don't understand! She doesn't do this for me; she doesn't do that for me." Listen closely. Reasons never change results. I will say it again. *Reasons never change results.* This means you can have all the best reasons in the world for not doing what the Bible says to do, but it still doesn't change the end result. You can have reasons why you don't have to love your spouse, but those reasons do not change the result of a bad marriage.

You can have reasons not to forgive—probably, really good ones. It could be someone who abused you when you were a child. That was wrong; it was unfair. You have great reasons not to forgive. Those reasons don't change the result. You still live with the bitterness, the anger, and the hurt that are eating you up from the inside out. They limit you in all of your relationships, and they hold you back in life.

Your great reasons do not excuse you from applying biblical principles that say to forgive. When you forgive, you release all that junk, and this allows you step into all that God wants for your life.

See, we have to learn to look beyond the reasons and apply the biblical principles to change results. If you look beyond the reasons why you don't have to love her, you start to love her unconditionally. This means *no conditions*; your love is not based on what she does. You pour into her like you did when you started dating. You begin to do all you can to win her heart. In a matter of time, she begins to love you back. She is now doing the things you wanted done. The two of you have stepped into a great marriage, by looking past the reasons, moving towards the results.

(One important exception: this never applies to a marriage with abuse.)

Love: It's a Choice

We as parents have to teach our children that love is a choice, not a feeling. You may not feel love towards your sibling, but that does not excuse you from loving them. This means treating them with kindness, sharing with them, giving to them, speaking only good about them, forgiving them, and working out your differences. Loving your siblings is not an option. You will grow up and love each other. Our kids are always told, "you are best friends for life."

The virtue of love needs to be placed in your kids' hearts from the time they are born. In a very real way, you are teaching them about marriage. Once you see it that way, it will change your attitude. Yes, your kids will fight, but do you teach them how to quickly work it out, how to forgive, forget, and restore the relationship?

Many parents let their kids be mad at each other for weeks, waiting for them to figure it out. They need you to train them, teach them, how not to let the sun go down on their anger (Ephesians 4:26). "Sorry kids, we aren't going to bed until this is resolved." Are you showing them each day how to give into the other, how to look for ways to be kind, and how to look for ways to love?

The Jar

The jar of character is an amazing tool for this. Our kids used to fight each other, battling to see who got to sit in the very back seat. They would practically run over each other to get there, followed by a long discussion about who went last, and whose turn it was.

One day, I told Baylor that, had he let Laken sit there, he would have gotten a marble. I then explained how that was love, and it was the right thing to do. Wouldn't you know, the next time, he let Laken sit there. Now we have a little problem of "No, you take the seat! No, you take the seat! No, I said you take the seat! Mom, Laken won't let me love him!"

Whenever our kids step out and do something unexpected, and do something really nice for one another, a marble is given. When they fight over stupid things or argue over nonsense, they lose a marble. We are teaching them that in life, there are things to get mad about and deal with—but most things in life aren't those things. Learn how to walk in love. Learn how to see the world from others' point of view. Learn how to do things to and for others that you want done for you.

Are you teaching your kids how to walk in love? Are you training them to be a great friend; to be a great spouse? If not, what changes need to be made now? Are you teaching them that love is a choice, and then teaching them how to choose it?

It Starts with You!

Love starts with you. They will learn what love is all about based upon how you love—how you respond to loved ones, how you deal with issues, and how you speak to and about others. All of your actions are teaching your kids what love is. How you treat their other parent is one of the major factors of what love becomes to them. Do you talk bad about your ex, do little mean things to annoy him or her? Your kids are watching. They see all of this. It is shaping and forming what love is. Your children learn more about love from watching you, then they ever will from you teaching them.

The Disclaimer:
Disclaimer to all single parents, divorced parents, and blended-family parents—over half of those reading this book. This chapter can be very hard for you to read because you don't have the kind of marriage we're talking about. You might feel like you have failed (you haven't), and that there is no hope (there is a lot of hope). Understand that your children can be just as successful. It will just take more work. It will be harder and take more time. I know it is not fair, but it is the truth.

You can sit around being mad at the injustice, or you can just deal with it. If you sit around waiting for life to be fair, you will never accomplish anything. It is important that you and your children realize that life is not, nor will it ever be, fair, but we always maximize whatever situation we are in.

Understand it is God's perfect plan for a man and woman to get married, love each other their entire life, have kids, and raise them up together. That is his perfect plan. If you have two people working towards that, loving each other, then that is the easiest road to raising great kids.

But, on a side note, if you are married to a bum who doesn't love you, isn't working, runs around, then having him around is doing more damage than good. Your son is learning how to be a husband from his example, and your daughter is learning what to expect from a husband from what you put up with.

Two people loving each other, married, raising kids is the perfect plan. If that is not your case, don't despair. Maybe you had a bad situation, or maybe you messed up or gave up. That's in the past, and that is where we'll leave it. We move onto the future. There is no condemnation in Christ! When you read this chapter, don't feel guilty. Instead, learn what you want in your next marriage. Learn what you want to instill in your kids for their marriage. It will help you understand what to look for in a spouse—to learn what is important. Pass that on to your kids.

Blended families—please learn from this chapter. Single moms, I want you to realize that God is the father to the fatherless. He has taken that place in your home. In many situations you can place God in the place of the husband. Apply what I talk about to Him.

Just don't get mad at the messenger (that is, Holly and Scot). We're passionate about this section, but don't allow our passion to make you feel bad. We will use phrases like "the most important thing to your children is mom and dad together." Yes, it is, but it didn't work out, now we move on. And your kids will be fine.

Single parents and divorced parents—please listen to this. As a single parent, you will nullify all of your good intentions and hard work with your children if you talk badly about their mother or father and don't love them the way God does. Not based on what he or she does, or does not do, but because they exist. If for nothing else, you love her because she is the most important and influential woman in your child's life. Or he is the most important and influential man in your child's life.

Think of it from a child's perspective: how much trust can he have in a father who talks down to their mom, who is rude to her, and who speaks negatively about her? How much trust can that child have in a mother who belittles, is rude to, or speaks bad about the most important man in their life? How much trust can the child have in a father who does things behind mom's back, a father who doesn't back her up but only puts her down? How can a child trust a man who does not love the most important woman in that child's life? How can a child trust a woman who does not love the most important man in that child's life?

All the fun time you spend with your kids and all your hard work to be a great father and a great mother might be wasted. You cannot be a great dad unless you love your children's mother. You cannot be a great mom unless you love your children's father. (This doesn't mean we don't take them to court for support to make sure they are taking up their end of the bargain. But the kids don't need to know any of those details.)

In this, know, that love conquers all. She may talk bad about you to the kids, but you keep on your course and speak only positive about her. He may put you down and may not pay support. You stay on your course. One day, the truth will be revealed to the kids. You back her up on things she wants done with the kids. You make sure the kids respect her and honor her. Teach your children to love their mom. You make sure your children respect him and love their dad.

Make sure they get gifts on holidays and birthdays for the other person. In doing these things, you are building trust in your children, but you are also building trust in your ex. So, when the time comes and you don't agree with a parenting direction, it is that love that you gave that will give you a window of opportunity to speak into their life.

Over the years, your love has built trust. You clearly have the best interests in mind for your child. Though you are divorced, it will be this trust that allows you to guide and steer the family towards God's plans. Besides, whatever the case, whatever the details of the divorce, the apostle Paul says we are to leave the past where it belongs—in the past—and we are to press forward to the future (Phil. 3:13).

For the Married Couples: Make Your Marriage a Decision

For many of us including myself, marriage was the right decision—the greatest thing ever to happen to me. I don't say that just to get the goodies, but Holly was the right choice. Some of you may feel that your marriage wasn't the right decision, and you shouldn't have married the person you share your life with.

What I am about to say isn't fair, but it is right. If you grab ahold of it, it will change your life. In our lives, there are times when we make right decisions, and that is great. My marriage was a right decision. But more importantly, there are times in our lives when we need to *make* our decisions right. I will say this one more time. Although we may have made a mistake, instead of throwing it away, it is our *responsibility* to make the mistake into the right choice.

Suppose you are in a marriage that is full of strife, bitterness, and fighting. But you have kids. Though the decision to get married may seem to be a wrong one, you now have the opportunity to *make* it right. You have the chance to make the wrong choice into the right choice. Choose, so that years down the road, you will celebrate your choice.

Many people have said that life is about making right decisions. But more importantly, it is about *making decisions right*.

Right now, it may not seem as if you made the right decision when you married the woman you married. But where life takes you from here is about making that decision right. See, you can spend time working on the marriage, reading books, getting tapes, going to marriage seminars, growing, and changing. You can invest time in making your marriage amazing. And in time, it will be.

Or you can spend the time trying to fix the results of what a divorce brings into your life, including time in courts, time with lawyers, working extra to pay support, and picking the kids up every other weekend. One way or the other, I guarantee you will spend time.

My own parents didn't have a perfect marriage. They fought a lot when I was growing up. They were two different people forced to live one life, as with any married couple. That "loving feeling" wasn't always there. But to them, divorce was never an option. I didn't go through the junk some of my friends went through—all the fear and worry. Instead, my parents got all the books and tapes on marriage they could find and went to all the seminars they could. They both worked hard at loving each other.

Today, 40 years later, they are best friends who are able to enjoy their family together and to look back at the huge mountain called marriage that they climbed together. The single greatest gift my parents ever gave me was their hard work to "make their decision right."

Can You Remember?

Go back with me to a time when you were a child. Mom and Dad are screaming at each other. Did you go into your room, pull the covers over your head, and cry yourself to sleep, praying that Mom and Dad would just love each other? Were you confused, upset, worried, and depressed, wondering what you did to cause this? And when the divorce did come, what happened to your entire world? It flipped upside down. You couldn't be secure in the world because your world had no security. You couldn't be you because you made no sense. The insecurity of your parents' marriage brought pain into your world.

Inside of each child is the need to know that mom and dad love each other. Your kids would give up everything they have, give all the toys back if mom and dad would just love each other. It is the most important need your children have. I have even counseled someone who said they would have given up the love their parents had for them for their parents to love each other.

You can give your kids the world, but the greatest gift would be to love your partner. This means, if you are married, you cannot be a great dad unless you are first a great husband. You also cannot be a great mom unless you are first a great wife.

This means that the husband-wife relationship has to be the priority relationship of the family. It is the heart of the family; it is what the children draw their security from. If the husband-wife relationship is not secure, the children will be insecure.

If kids go off to school and in their hearts have no doubt of Mom and Dad's love for each other, imagine their sense of security. They know that divorce is never an option and that their mom and dad will do anything to work things out even if they do fight once in a while. Guess what? With that worry off their shoulders, kids can focus on school, friends, and being a kid. They can go forth confidently into the world.

As husband and wife, we will fight, and there is nothing wrong with them seeing that once in a while. They learn how to work out disagreements in love, how to stick to commitments and never give up, how to love each other through disagreements, and how to forgive and forget. These life lessons must be placed in their warehouse.

Your children learn what love is by observing your relationship. When you tell your child to love their brother, the child might answer, "he did this and that to me." You say that it doesn't matter what he did; that you need to always love him (look beyond the reason, so you can get the result). They will need to *choose* to love him.

But if "Daddy fell out of love with Mommy," it won't make any sense when you say, "You have to love your brother, but you don't have to love your mother." They grow up confused about what love really is. Why do they have to be nice when you're not?

Divorce: Fish or Cut Bait

What if Mom and Dad are constantly talking divorce? Nobody in the family knows if the marriage will last another day. And the fights are *intense*. This child takes the worry of what his world could become out into the world with him and is never free to just be a kid.

In most ways, it is better to just divorce than to stay together and keep talking divorce. It's a very slow, emotional torture to the child. At least if you do divorce, it's over. The child doesn't have to worry anymore. We, of course, are not saying to divorce, our point is to *stop talking about it*. Instill security into your kid's heart, that mom and dad are together forever.

See Past the Divorce and Look into The Future.

(If you are divorced skip this section. Once again, no condemnation.)

I don't think most people really think about what waits for them on the road of divorce. They don't think through what it will be like to have their children call another man Dad; another woman Mom. What will it be like if the new father has different attitudes and views about raising their children? What if the new mom decides to move to another state? Then they would only see their kids in the summers and on certain holidays. Another man would do their job of fathering; another woman playing the part of the mother. Stealing their time with those kids—time they could never get back.

It's like I heard one little girl say when her parents got divorced. "I went from saying good night to my dad at night to saying good-bye."

If right now, the decision to marry your spouse doesn't seem like the right one, think about what it would be like to spend half of your holidays away from your children. You'd go from tucking them into bed every night to seeing them every other weekend. You might no longer be a part of their world. Instead, you might get to peek into their world every so often. Imagine how hard it would be to start a new family while supporting your old family. The state will tell you to pay support, and it will seem like a lot, but in reality, it won't be enough.

And what will it be like when your kids say, "Dad, please stay here tonight—please stay home." You'll have to explain to them that their home isn't Daddy's home anymore. With tears in their eyes, they might ask, "But, Daddy, who will protect us, who will watch over the house, who will be there if we get scared at night?" Explain to them then why Daddy doesn't love Mommy anymore.

If at all possible, wouldn't it be better to make that decision right. You know, the one that you made during your marriage vows—the decision to love your husband and your wife "till death do us part?"

This being a parenting book, I can't spend all the time needed to help you have a great marriage. That is your job. You need to go to marriage seminars, read books, and listen to tapes. Learn how to be a great husband; how to be a great wife. If you won't do that for yourself, do it for your children. because it is so important to them. Once again, the single greatest thing you could ever give your children is a great marriage.

You Are a Family Before You Have Kids

Many people consider themselves a family after they have children. You hear new parents say, "We are a family now." No, you were already a family. That type of thinking is one of the main reasons for divorce. We lower the value of the husband-wife relationship. When the husband-wife relationship is not the most valuable relationship in the home, it doesn't get the attention it needs to be successful. That simple thought of "now we are a family" is the reason for so many divorces.

You were a family before the kids ever came. A healthy family says that "the kids are a welcome addition to the family; they do not make us a family."

Let Me Show You How God Views Marriage
Ephesians 5:31 (New King James Version) *For this reason a man shall leave his father and mother and be joined to his wife, and the two shall become one flesh.* [a]

Now, a lot of pastors will stop right there, but you gotta go on to Verse 32, because he is not necessarily just talking about husband-wife relationships.

Ephesians 5:32 (New King James Version) *This is a great mystery, but I speak concerning Christ and the church.*

God is trying to explain the importance of Christ and the church. God says the husband-wife relationship is so important, so valuable that *the only thing he can compare it to is Christ and the church.* It is time we see marriage like God does. When we see marriage the way God sees it, when we value it as he does, it changes how we treat it.

Quick Teaching on Values
Everything in life has a value to you. For those things that are most valuable, you will spend your time, energy, and resources. For

those things that are less valuable, you will find excuses for why you don't spend time, money, and resources.

In life, whenever you overvalue something, you lose out on the things you undervalue. It is the *Bob Barker Principle*. What happens on The Price Is Right when you overvalue something
By just a dollar? You lose it. Same with life. Everything in life has a value, but when you overvalue something, you lose those things you undervalued.

Isaiah says if you have God's thoughts, you have His ways. If you have His value system, you get the life He intended for you. When you have the world's value systems, you end up with regrets in your life. To live a life of no regrets, you must get your values in order.

Let's look at an example. Golf has value. But when it becomes more valuable than your marriage, you lose out on the marriage God wants you to have. Because golf is so valuable to you, you'll find the time to make it to tee time. You're going to find the four hours-a-week to do it, and you're going to find the time to buy the two-thousand-dollar golf clubs because golf has value. I am not saying golf doesn't have value, but the husband-wife relationship should have more value.

You haven't had the time to go to the marriage seminars, and you haven't had the time to read any books on being a better husband. But you've read every issue of Golf Digest for the last 18 months. You have time to make a tee time, but you don't make a wife time. You have to hit a bucket of balls every day because you want to be successful at golf. Why can't you take an hour a day and really talk to your wife? This would help you become a successful husband. You have to get a lesson to fix your swing, but your marriage has been broken for 5 years, and you don't have time to go for counseling.

At the end of your life, I guarantee that a great marriage will bring you far more joy and happiness than all the great golf games you can imagine. If your life's values are messed up, you'll miss out on the marriage God wants you to have.

We have to see marriage the way God does. It is one of the most important things here on earth. You wouldn't throw it away, you wouldn't give up on it as God wouldn't give up on the church, and He wouldn't throw away the church. That is its place in the home and family. That is where our time and energy should go.

To some men, cable TV is more valuable than their marriage. Let me prove it. Your marriage has been broken for years and you don't have the time to go to marriage seminars. You don't have the $100 to pay for the marriage seminar. You don't have the time to read books and listen to tapes on being a great spouse.

But God forbid the cable TV goes out. You get out all the books you can find. You have to see if you can get that thing fixed *right now*. You research on the internet. You call the cable counselor (tech support). You wait on hold an hour, waiting to talk to this important person who will change your life. They say we will have a technician out there between 9am-5pm (I hate that). You call the job, where you can never get time off, and say you can't come in today. The cable guy says it will cost $150, and, somehow, you find the money to get it fixed. If you had that same attitude towards your marriage, it would be fixed in short amount of time.

A Quick Motivator
Maybe a great marriage isn't motivation enough for you. You just don't buy it. We are hoping you can see the impact on your children, and this will motivate you to value the husband- wife relationship. If we remember that the husband-wife relationship is the universe and the center of the world that the child knows, then we are going to work our hardest to keep it going. Because if it falls apart, the children's world does too.

All that love that you have for your children, knowing how badly you just want to give them everything and devote everything to them, should help you remember that by devoting yourself to your marriage, you are giving everything to them. You are making their universe a solid and secure place where they can live and be confident in themselves and grow.

Let Us Give You Some Parenting Basics on Marriage That Will Change Your Life

There are two things which, if allowed, can hurt, hold back, or even destroy your marriage. The first is not making the husband-wife relationship priority in the home. The second is creating a child-centered home.

Child-Centered (Laken the King is Born, Let the Angels Sing)
When our first child (the chosen one) was born, he was our savior. We forgot all about the husband-wife relationship because glorious Laken was our world. We stopped having dates because of Laken. Laken became the center of the universe. Everything revolved around his needs.

As soon as he cried, we picked him up and rocked him for hours. Our job as parents was to provide him a world of complete happiness, meeting all of his needs right when he had them. Every night, we would pat his little booty and rub his back for hours trying to get him to go to sleep. (Sometimes at three o'clock in the morning, I found myself patting his back a little harder than normal, nearly bouncing him in his bed.) I waited for the prince to go to sleep. He would finally close his eyes, and as I began to walk away, he would cry again.

One time I got so frustrated that I took him for a drive because he always fell asleep in the car. Sure enough, he was out. But by the time I got into the house, he was awake again. I then had an answer, as if from God, and I put his car seat on the dryer and turned it on, recreating the car experience. This only annoyed the chosen one.

We began to have little Prince Abu sleep in our bed where we could instantly and throughout the night meet his needs whenever he wanted. Waking up every hour on the hour and being afraid of rolling over and squishing the prince, I never got a good night sleep (let alone any nighttime goodies from the Missus!) Finally, I cried out to God, "I'm tired, I'm horny, and I'm mad. Take me now God or give me another way." Holly and I began to read all the books we could. We found out how very wrong we were. We were setting Laken up for failure.

Children for whom the world revolves around struggle in every area of adulthood. All because their parents didn't teach them what life is about. Life isn't all about you, it is about others. The world isn't there to give to you and meet your needs. You are not the world—you are part of the world. Children who don't learn this grow up to be very selfish people who are unable to have any quality relationships. They are still taking from their parents. They can't seem to be responsible for anything because they were never given or trained to be responsible. Their marriages hardly ever work, because the theme of their marriages is, "meet my needs."

Children are not the center of the family universe; they are a part of it. They are expected to give into it.

Me, Me, Me, and Me!
When you become child-centered, the child grows up with a "me" attitude. What can the family give to me? The family isn't meeting my needs. What about me? The family becomes nothing more than a place that they *get from*, not *give into*. The child grows up to resent this family because all the love in the world can't fill up this empty feeling when you don't love back.

When the husband-wife relationship is priority, we teach the child a "we" attitude. You are a welcome *member* of this family; *you are not the family*. The child becomes family minded.

This is critical: because the marriage is the foundation of the home, children come to understand that the husband-wife relationship is the most important relationship in the home. All other relationships are subject to it. Understand that the quality of the parent-child relationship depends on the quality of the relationship between Mom and Dad.

You need to show your kids that Mom and Dad's relationship is number one in the home. Mom and Dad are the heart of the family. If the heart isn't doing good, the family isn't doing good.

Here are the things to do that will keep you out of a child-centered home, and will keep the family with the attitude that Mom and Dad's relationship is number 1:

Number 1 – Mom and Me Time
You make sure that when Dad gets home, he spends the first 15 minutes with Mom. This is called *Mom and Me Time*. Since the husband-wife relationship is most important, it has to be treated that way. The wife gets the first fruits of the night. I realize the kids are pulling on Dad, wanting Dad to play. Dad says "I love you so much that I'm going to talk to Mom. Dad wants to find out about her day and what is going on her life."

They want Dad to come play with them, but on the inside, a need is being met. *My dad loves my mom.* Mom and Dad's relationship is most important thing. A lot of husbands and wives say, "we do that when the kids go to bed." No, no, I want you to get this in your heart. It is vital that your children *see* Mom and Me time; they see Dad and Mom sitting on the couch sharing their day.

Men, if you are not good communicators, then become one. It is not that hard to do. Get the books and the tapes. Communicating is a learned skill, just like fishing or basketball. Learn how and become great at it.

Number 2 – Let's Go Out on a Date

Once a week Dad plans a date with Mom. He takes her out for a night with just the two of them. He develops that relationship because there will come a day when it is just the two of you, and if you haven't built the relationship by then, you will go through the empty nest syndrome, where many end up in divorce. Kid yourself all you want, but a divorce is just as painful to your 25-year-old as it is to your 5-year-old. If you take Mom out once a week, the kids might ask if they can come. Say, "I love you too much to take you with us."

Don't have the time? Find the time. We are talking about the most important thing in your kids' lives. You find the time to watch TV every day, find the time to watch a game on the weekend, and find the time to golf with your buddies. These are all things that will never give you as much joy as a great marriage.

You may have the lame excuse you don't have the money. My parents didn't have the money, but they still went out. They went to the park and talked, or they shared a dessert at Denny's. Don't have money for a babysitter? Cancel the cable TV, stop drinking soda, or stop buying fast food during the week. This is more important.

If you can't do it for you, or for her, then do it for the kids. Tell your kids, "I love you so much that I'm not taking you with me."

This definitely goes for new moms. You have to have time out with your husband, even if it is just for a couple of hours, that first month. Set the standard—*we will have time for a date*.

A Date Is Not:
1.   Staying home and having a date at home. That is every night. A date is going out. When you are home, the kids are bugging you, you still have the responsibility of the children hanging over your head. It is far, far from a date.
2.   Going out with other couples. I encourage you to do his once in a while, but it never takes the place of your date night.

When you go out with other couples, you are working on your relationship with those other couples, not on the husband-wife relationship.

3. Just going to a movie. That is not a date. A date has to have an element of communication in it. Make sure the date has at least an hour where you talk to each other and share with each other.

A date "Anderson style," is a time alone, where the relationship grows. Judge your dates, not by the time spent, but by the relationship that comes out of that time. If no relationship is coming out of your time, then change how you spend the time. Tweak it until your relationship is growing each time you go out.

Number 3 – Let's Learn How to Be Married
Make sure you go to a marriage seminar every year. Why? Because marriage is the most important thing you do. Why not be the best at it? Learn all you can. Continue to grow and to change. The kids may say, "come on skip it, spend time with us." On the outside they want you home, but on the inside, you are teaching them priceless lessons—to be good at anything, you must work. And you work the hardest for things that are most important. Your children will get the greatest gift you could give them: a great marriage.

You should be reading at least a year on becoming a better spouse. You might say, "Pastor, that is a lot." Not really. Think about the fact that you read 14 love novels last year, you read 12 issues of People, you read 12 issues of Field and Stream, 12 issues of Golf Digest. You read a lot—you just didn't read a lot of important things. You can tell me how to catch a huge bass, but you can't tell me how to catch your wife's heart. You can tell me how to hit a draw on a golf ball, but you can't tell me how to meet the needs of your wife. Which of the two will give you a better life?

Number 4 – Let's Go on a Trip
Make sure you and your wife go on a trip alone twice a year. Get away and just enjoy each other. It doesn't have to be for ten days—

a couple of days is fine. It doesn't have to be expensive. Holly and I used to go to Laughlin. Not to gamble, but because we didn't have the money, but because rooms were $19 a night and the third night was free. Steak dinners were $4.

Get away time is time for just the two of you. You will come back so refreshed and ready to be an even better parent. Once again, your kids will be excited because you love each other.

Number 5 – Let's Try and Agree
One horse can pull a ton; two horses can pull four tons. The Bible says that when two come into agreement on anything, it will be done. One of the biggest mistakes parents make is not being in agreement.

Agreement is one of the most important things that you can have in the home. Kids are so smart they will play you; they know if Mom says no, I just go to Dad. The child learns to work the parents to get what they want, not what they need in life. Lack of agreement brings division to the home and to the most important relationship.

My kids know that if Mom says no, the answer is no. If you come to me and try and trick me, asking me if you can do something that Mom has already gave you an answer to, we will move right to Chapter 10 (discipline). Agreement is important in my home. Mom and Dad will always back each other up.

If you ever find yourself in a place where you two don't agree, don't ever talk about it in front of the kids. Go off somewhere and talk about it. If the other parent changes their mind, let them come out and be the one that changed their mind. Don't play the game "Dad saved the day; he got the kids what they wanted."

Parental agreement is more important than being right. The kids have to see that you are on the same page. They need to know that you will always back each other up.

This also goes for a kid talking back to a parent. There are times I'm caught up in the moment of training a child, and I don't notice that one of my children are talking disrespectful to me. Holly says, "You don't talk to your dad that way." Mom is watching my back. And God forbid my kids ever, ever talk back to Mom. That is the love of my life; she is the most important thing to me. No one talks that way to her.

I remember at age 20 I said something rude to my mom. My Dad grabbed me, walked me up to a wall, and said you don't ever talk to my wife that way. He didn't say your mom. No, he was not defending my mom; *he was defending his wife*, the love of his life.

When we back each other up and are in agreement, the kids are able to see how much we mean to each other. They see the value of the husband-wife relationship.

Number 6 – Voice Our Commitment
Your kids need to hear you say how much you love each other. They need to hear you say how important you are to each other. Let's say that you're driving along, and you say, "Kids, Dad is so lucky to have an amazing wife like your mom. You have the best Mom in the world."

Yes, we will have fights in front of the kids, and we will probably even say things we don't mean. This is one of the reasons they need to hear us say things we do mean (or pretend we mean before we actually come to believe it). Look for opportunities to tell your kids what a great Dad they have, what an amazing husband you have.

You should point your kids toward the good side of the other parent. Teach them how to look past our faults and see the good. Sure, Dad has his faults, but he has so many great characteristics. The key to a happy home in the teenage years is a home that focuses on the good. I don't know how, but when we say goodbye, our kids, scream, "Bye Mom, best Mom in the world. Bye Dad, best Dad in the world." They speak that over and over and over, and it becomes embedded in their heart. I have the best parents in the world. I am so lucky.

There are a lot of great parents out there whose kids can't see their parent's good side. They hate their home and hate their parents. Why? Because Mom and Dad did not teach them to see the good and focus on the good.

You never, ever include your kids in your fights. They have enough to worry about without having to worry about your marriage. When you speak bad about the other parent to your children, you break trust. If Dad will talk down about Mom to me, I wonder what he says about me. No, even in the midst of a fight, you must find the way to still talk great about mom.

Number 7 – Show Affection
They act like they hate it. "Daaaaad! Stop, don't kiss Mom. That is *gross*." Yet it is so important for them to see affection. It is the outside demonstration of what they desire Mom and Dad to have on the inside. They desire Mom and Dad to be in love, just like the movies.

Number 8 – Divorce Is Not an Option
Many divorces have happened, not because two people wanted it, but because they spoke it. They spoke insecurity into the relationship, and, in time, it came to pass. Words are seeds. Once you say it, the seed is planted. Once you say I am going to take a break, I am going to take a little time away, a seed of insecurity has been planted.

Your spouse begins to doubt the relationship. During every fight, your kids wonder if this *the one*. It brings so much insecurity into their world. They can become emotionally consumed with worry about the most important relationship in their life —your marriage.

Yes, your kids will see you fight; that is fine. But it has to be in their heart that Mom and Dad will always work it out. That is what love is. *Love never fails.*

Holly and I have a great relationship, but on some days, we are going to bring some heat. That's just the way it is. We try very hard not to fight in front of the kids, but I occasionally say something stupid. It is who I am. And we may have a fight in front of the kids. But divorce is never an option! A fight in front of the kids that talks divorce, can greatly affect them. But a fight where they sit back and watch and see how the two of you work it out, that is a great life lesson.

Number 9 – Mom Deserves the World, So Does Dad
For some, Christmas time means, "Mom and Dad are not going to get gifts, we are going to just give to the kids." Mistake. That is child centered. Yes, on the outside the kids are excited to get what they want, but on the inside, they are not getting what they need. They need to see how important Mom and Dad are to each other. They need to see Dad give Mom the amazing necklace and Dad receive the power tool he has been talking about for months. You must show the kids how valuable each of you are to the other.

If I spend $150 on each kid, then I better spend at least that on Mom. The kids need to see how valuable Mom is. They've got the best Mom in the world. Their Dad is so amazing, he is willing to receive nothing for Christmas for the kids' sake. But we love him too much to let that happen.

Sure, on the outside, your kids would love to get more toys, but on the inside, they need to see how much Mom and Dad love each other.

It is very important that you take the kids out and teach them how to shop for Mom and shop for Dad. We will talk more about this next chapter. Understand that I don't need their $10 gift, but I do need their heart. I need them to love me back.

Questions for Review:

1. What is Love? What changes do you need to make to be a great example of what love is to your children?

2. What is the most important relationship in the home and why?

3. What is child-centered parenting, and why is it dangerous to the family unit?

Your Scenario for Discussion:

Your 12-year-old tells you to #$%# Off!

This Week at Home:

Work on demonstrating affection for your spouse in front of the kids. Note their reactions.

CHAPTER 6:
The Language of Love/Loving your Parents is not an Option

We are in France and my goal is to find Le-Toilet, so I can wee-wee. The problem is this: no one speaks my language. I can scream my language, yell it, even slow it down. Still I'm standing there dancing in place, frustrated, because no can understand me.

This is how many relationships feel. You feel like you are loving the other person, giving your life to him or her, and he or she seems to be nothing but ungrateful. All they do is talk about how you never love them, and they give the world to you. The problem is both people are right.

Both people love the other person, but they are not speaking the right language. They are speaking their own love language and not the love language of the other. And no matter how you speak it, the other person just can't understand. This leaves you frustrated and mad, but it also leaves them feeling the same way.

If I wanted to be successful in France, I would need to learn the language of those I'm around. It's the same with love. To be successful in relationships, you have to learn to speak their language. In this chapter, we will discuss the five love languages. We will discover what your love language is and also your spouse's. If your kids are old enough, we will discover their love language. You will see a dramatic difference in all of your relationships when you start speaking the language they understand.

Before we get to the languages, I want you to picture a storage tank inside of you. This is called your love tank. As you receive love, this tank fills up, and as you give it, it empties. God's plan is for us to have balance. Balance means that people are giving into us and we in turn are giving into people. When we don't have balance, our lives go in one of two ways.

One just gives love. She finds herself giving to the lazy husband and giving all day at work. She is a doormat to all those in her life. Her tank is often empty before she even gets to work. It takes effort just to keep from going off at every person throughout the day. She finds herself snapping at the waitress over Ranch dressing. She snaps at the other driver for getting in front of her and costing her nearly one second of drive time. By the time she gets home, she has nothing left inside. She finds herself snapping at the kids over nothing, going off on the husband at the slightest whim. She goes to bed feeling guilty for what she did and said all day.

This person needs to expect to be loved by those around her. This person needs to get the books *Boundaries*, *Self Matters*, and Scot's series *DNA of Relationships*. Since this is a parenting book, these matters are outside the scope of this book.

The other out-of-balance person is "all about me." He just takes love. "Make me dinner (even though she worked all day). Do my laundry. Get this. Do that"—while he just sits in front of the TV, never meeting her needs. (I know I stereotyped a little, but you can switch it up. A lot of times, it is the female that is just taking.) This person feels horrible inside and thinks, "If I can just take more love, I will feel better." The problem is, the love inside them spoils. No matter how much love they get, it is never enough. They don't understand that love isn't activated until it is given away. That is God's natural process.

Where we receive love, we can give love. When we have this balance in our lives, we feel our best. We feel alive.

The marriage God has for you is one where you are giving and receiving love. You get two people, each filling up the other's tank. But you have to give that love in the other person's love language. You cannot fill their love tank with your love language; it has to be theirs.

The same goes for your kids. You don't love the kids the same way you receive love. You have to learn to love them in the very individual way in which they receive love.

Let's Discuss the Love Languages

(This next section is a brief overview of Gary Chapman's book *The Five Love Languages*. I strongly suggest you read this book. Reading it changed our lives.)

Because a particular love language is how we receive love personally, or individually, we tend to think everyone else receives love the same way. But in reality, that's probably not true. You may be doing all kinds of things for your wife, and after a while, you might think, "What the heck? She is so unappreciative."

At the same time, she is upset with you, because in her mind, you never show her love! In reality, it's not that you don't love her. You just aren't loving her the way she needs to be loved.

Let me give you an example of how this works in the parent/child relationship: A dad comes home and says, "Son, I bought you a wooden glider today. Why don't you go out front and fly it around?" The dad who shows his love for others with gift-giving does so because that's how he best receives love. When someone gives something to him, he feels loved by that particular action. So, to show love, he gives gifts. And he feels that his actions are indications of his love.

But suppose this dad's son, on the other hand, likes quality time. Having quality time with someone he loves makes him feel loved by that person. The gift of the wooden glider doesn't mean as much to him. But he would give anything in the world if Dad would take a walk with him and talk with him—or come outside and fly the glider with him!

If Dad doesn't recognize his son's "love language," he will go through life feeling like he gave his son the world but was never appreciated for the love he showed. And the son will grow up having never felt loved by his dad. Once again, it wasn't that his dad wasn't giving love to his son; it just wasn't the right type of love.

Here's another example. Maybe a dad feels love best through spending quality time together. He says, "Hey, Son, let's go for a walk and get some ice cream." But his son never really wants to go. So, the dad feels like his son doesn't want to spend time with him and is rejecting his father's love.

In the meantime, the son, who is best loved by acts of service, feels rejected by his father. This son would love it if Dad would come out and work on his bike with him, help him build a fort, or help the coach of his baseball team. When it doesn't happen, that boy may grow up feeling like Dad wasn't there for him, which is untrue. Dad was there—just not in the way the son wanted him to be.

Many parents are frustrated because their kids act like their parents don't love them. If that describes you, it's not necessarily that you're not trying to love your kids, but it's probably true that you're not loving them in the way they need it most. In other words, you're not communicating your love in the most effective way for them.

What good is giving something to someone else if it is something he or she doesn't really need? If we're going to communicate love effectively, we need to find out what our loved ones need and then give it to them. As parents, we need to learn the languages of love and find out what our spouse and each of our children's primary love languages are. Then we can make sure we are communicating love to them through those languages.

The Five Languages of Love

There are five primary love languages, and here is a brief overview. (But, please, get the book. It is more comprehensive, and if you want to be really good at something, you need to fully understand it.)

Show Me the Money

Love language number one is what we call the "show-me-the-money" or the "gift-giving language." Some people feel most loved by receiving gifts. These are the people who, when they get a birthday card, first shake the card to see if money drops out. What the card says inside doesn't matter as much as what falls out of it!

Now, to "speak" this language to your kids, you don't have to buy huge, expensive gifts. You could just get them something that says, "Today I thought of you." Right now, in my eleven-year-old's life, this is his main love language. It's not that all kids don't want gifts, but to some kids, gifts tend to be a little more special. I can come home with gifts for all my kids, but Laken carries his gift around for days. He shows everyone what Mom got him. Heath, my ten-year-old, plays with his gift for ten minutes, and then off he goes. He's very thankful for the gift, but the gift itself doesn't communicate love to him like it does to Laken.

Do Something for Me, Anything

Love language number two is what I call "What have you done for me lately?" or "acts of service." This love language is communicated when you do something unexpected or outside the norm for someone. For example, if I come home and my wife has taken out the garbage for me, that is love communicated by an act of service. Because I am an acts-of-service person, that blesses me. She did something for me that she knew I would appreciate, and that makes me feel loved.

For your kids, this particular love language may be communicated by fixing their bike, building a tree house, or in their teen years, helping them work on their car. Some of my greatest moments as a teen were the times my dad would spend working on my car with me.

As I said, I am an acts-of-service guy, so this love language comes naturally to me. Some dads may miss it because they're gift-givers, so they'll say, "Hey, Son, I will pay someone to fix that." The dad feels like he's showing love to the son, but if the son's love language is acts of service, the father is missing an opportunity to love his son effectively.

Now, you may not be good with cars or tools, and paying someone is the right route to go. But you must find other ways to do something for your child. You may coach his little league team or wash his car for him unexpectedly. (And don't pay someone to wash it. It's a love gift from you, so *you* do it.) To a gift-giver, that may sound stupid. His attitude is, "Why do it when I can pay someone to do it for me?" Stupid or not, your acts of service mean more to this child than your gifts.

Quality Time
Love language number three involves "quality time." Some people love to just sit and talk and share their life. Quality time requires that you give yourself to the conversation, you listen closely and give the appropriate responses. Giving time is a factor in showing love through quality time but realize that you don't need three hours at a time to show love. You may spend only ten or twenty minutes, but to that person, those few minutes made his or her whole day.

A child whose primary love language is quality time needs time each day when Mom and Dad listen to him. A ten-minute walk, sitting out on the swing, or driving to the store may be all you need. So, if your love language is acts of service and your child's is quality time, you could go out and wash his car if you want. But he or she will think, "Thanks, Dad, but I would rather that you just talked to me. I can wash my own car, but I can't have a conversation with my dad without you."

Words of Encouragement
Love language number four is "words of encouragement" or "affirmation. For this kind of child, when you say, "You are so good at that," it lights up their countenance (while other kids just say, "I know"). If your daughter's language is words of encouragement, you could tell her, "That dress really looks amazing on you" and that one little phrase will fill her "love tank" for the whole day.

This love language is simple to communicate. Just look for areas in which to encourage your kids. You don't want to flatter them, but you do want to find sincere ways to say, "You're great at that." I believe Heath, our ten-year-old, is motivated by this love language. When I say, "Son, you are so good at gymnastics! You're a natural," he gets this half smile on his face and gives me an embarrassed little nod. But then he walks away with a skip in his step. On the other hand, I can tell Laken, "You are very good at baseball," and he looks at me and says, "I know, Mom."

Showing Affection (Not Sex)
The last language of love is physical touch and closeness, or affection. To some people, a big hug, a hand on the shoulder, or an arm around them during a movie fills them right up with love. A person who's motivated by touch also loves just to spend time with someone he loves. What makes this different from quality time is that you don't have to talk to communicate love. You can just be around each other. You could be cleaning the garage while your son is working on his bike. You're not having some deep conversation; you're just near each other. This time spent together means the world to this child.

Note to Husbands (Sorry)—

This language is not about sex, so if touching your wife is about getting sex, then you are not loving her in her love language.

If physical touch and closeness describes your child's love language, plan time when you can just be near him or her and give this child the extra hugs he or she needs.

As you read this, you might be thinking, "My kids have all these love languages. They want the gifts, the service, the time, the words, and the touch—they want it all!" In some sense, this is true. You have to realize that your child's true love language won't really emerge until they're about eight years old. Your kids need to be loved in all these ways, but your job as a parent is to find the one or two ways that are especially meaningful to them.

Study these languages, knowing that your kids possess a need for each one, but one or two of them will be the most important to them as they get older.

Your goal is to be affluent in all the languages but also teaching your kids each language. What a head start on life you will give them if they can speak any of the languages at any time!

I See Why You Make Me So Mad
After you understand the five languages of love, you can see why so many fights and arguments happen in relationships over the years.

My wife, for example, is a quality time person, with a secondary language of physical touch and closeness. (I was genuinely surprised when I discovered that physical touch wasn't all about sex. I wanted to add love language number six—sex—this being all men's primary love language.) My love language is acts of service and gift-giving. When Holly buys me something and cleans the house? Man, I feel loved!

Before we read the love language book, we misread each other's efforts.

I would come home from work at least once a week with some sort of gift for her, and she would say, "That's nice. Thank you," and then sort of toss it aside. That annoyed me. She would then follow me throughout the house, talking to me while I cleaned up, put things away, and fixed things—until she would get mad because I wasn't listening to her. At that point, I would get mad because she seemed unappreciative of all the things I was doing for her.

On the weekends, Holly would want to do what I thought were some of the dumbest things ever. "Hey," she'd say, "why don't we drive to Payson?" (Payson is a town about a two-hour drive away.) When I would ask why, she'd say, "I don't know. Let's just have lunch up there."

I would, of course, respond, "No, let's just drive right up the street, have lunch, and come home, clean the house, and wash some white t-shirts." You see, Holly wanted that closeness of just sitting and talking in the car all the way. To me, that's what my version of what hell would be—just one long drive...

When you understand and begin to communicate these love languages, they will change your life. You'll understand your wife's language, your husband's language, your kids' language, and maybe even your boss's language. If you learn, for example, that your boss's love language is gift-giving, you could give a little extra gift on Boss's Day or on his or her birthday.

If it's acts of service, you can do things beyond what is expected of you in your job description. You could clean your boss's office, or you could carry his or her things to the car. And if your boss's language is physical touch, you could just hold him or her for long periods of time! Remember, a pat on the backside can sometimes go a long way. (All kidding aside, please leave that physical touch language alone in the workplace!)

What I'm trying to say is that you need to use these love languages to communicate effectively with your kids and with those closest to you. Learn how to nourish those relationships with their lifeblood: communication.

Learning to communicate correctly teaches your children the love and security they need to have a healthy, trusting relationship with you. Remember, communication isn't always just about the words you say; it's about your actions, too. When you begin to understand your children's love language, then you can truly communicate love to them, which, after all, is the highest goal of being a great parent!

Let's close with this: it is great we are talking about loving our kids, but it is critical that they learn to love you back. You need to teach them, show them, and then help them love you in the way you receive love.

Love Must Be Given

I have seen many parents really pour their hearts into loving their kids, giving them the world. And I have seen those kids grow up miserable, hate their parents, want to have nothing to do with them. What went wrong? They never taught their kids to love back. It is very important that parents love their kids, but maybe even more important, they teach their kids how to love back.

Let us give you the main areas. They may also be other ways you may think of in your home that your kids need to love you back. We are instilling the idea that love is something given. It will be a major part of their character, and one of the main driving forces that carries them to success in all the relationships in their life. It will be this that brings peace, joy, and happiness because we have taught them how to do what they were created to do.

1. Obedience is Love
God said if you love me, you will follow my commandments. We are a picture in our children's lives of what God will be in their adult lives. To paint the proper picture, we need to teach them that obedience is love. If we want our kids to love God, then as they grow up, we show them that love is obedience.

You give love to Mom when you clean up your toys like she asked you to. You give love to Mom when you come when she calls you, and you say, 'Yes, Mom.' You love your father when do what he asks you to do, the first time he asks it. That is loving back. Mom and Dad do so many things for you, we ask that you do this for us, that is, be obedient.

Doing what I ask with a happy heart is love. When you do what I ask, but stomp your feet, grumble, complain, and slam doors—that is not love. Parents, like God, look at the heart. If the heart was not obedient, neither were you. If you love me, you will do what I ask, and you will do it with a smile on your face. I refuse to raise a son who is mad whenever he has to love his wife, upset when he has to do things for her. I expect him to have a smile on his face, to be excited to love others. I put that in him by accepting nothing less. *You will love me, and you will be happy about it.*

2. How You Talk to Me Is Love
The way you talk to me – your tone of voice, how you respond to me—shows love. Loving me means you don't talk rudely to me, either in your words or in your tone. You can disagree with me, and we can talk about it, but your tone and your words need to always be in love.

Parents, how many fights have you gotten into with your spouse because of your tone of voice and the wrong, hurtful words that were said? Couldn't the disagreement have been settled a lot easier had you gone to them in love, watched what you said, and used wisdom to guide the disagreement away from a fight and into a peaceful resolution? That is what you are teaching them. Put this in their hearts, and you will save them many fights in their lifetime.

3. How You Talk About Me Is Love

Love means you don't talk bad about me. Husbands, wives, exes, and children—all of the above. Your kids are never allowed to talk bad about the other parent. It is your job to make sure of this. Now, Dad may be doing something that is hurtful, so they come to Mom, looking for resolution. Okay, we can counsel you through that. That is totally different from, "I can't stand Mom. She is so mean." You, as a parent, know the difference.

Is your child coming to you out of a heart of love, or because they're not getting what they want, or not getting to do what they want? Your goal is to teach them unconditional love, meaning *love without conditions*. You love Mom because she exists. You love Dad because he exists. You are constantly pointing your kids toward the good things in life. "You know your Mom loves you very much. She wants what is best for you. She takes you shopping. She buys you things. She sometimes doesn't get to do what she wants because she's taking care of you. Your mom ..." The list goes on and on.

You are raising a child who, when he gets married, goes for counseling to help solve the problem, rather than spend time bickering (making the problem worse). He learns how to make the relationship better, rather than just complain his life away, stuck in the same mess.

4. Giving Gifts on Special Occasions Shows Love

Gifts and cards are not an option but a requirement. Your kids are expected from age three on to get you something nice for Mother's Day, Father's Day, for birthdays, and Christmas. Obviously, our expectations change according to their age. But they love you by making these times special. You should take your kids out and make sure they get the other parent something nice for all holidays, out of their own money. Love is not an option. Love is something you practice. (If your ex doesn't do it for you, then you take your kids out and have them do it for you.) Let your kids pick out the card, then make sure they fill it out.

By the time your kids are twelve, they are expected to really put some thought into holidays, making those times special. They pick out the special card, and they take time to put their feelings onto those cards. Your kids then will spend their lifetime loving you on special events. But even more importantly, they will make special events important in the lives of their spouse and children.

6. Be Angry but Sin Not
Walking around mad at for a week because they were grounded is not an option. A wise man is happy with discipline and learns from it. I don't want to raise a fool. Your kids don't take anger to bed with them. They need to realize it was their actions, not yours, that got them in trouble. "You are blaming the wrong person. Being mad at me is not an option. Put a smile on your face and get over it."

My parents would say, "You have about thirty minutes to get happy." If not, we moved to Chapter 10. I got happy real quick. We don't want to raise kids who grow up pouting when things don't go their way. They become adults who are mad for weeks at their spouse. That anger will eat them up and destroy their lives from the inside out. Love is learning how to deal with that anger, get over it, forgive, and move on.

7. Helping You Around the House Is Love
Chores are not an option. They are how children learn love. We work very hard to put food on the plate, a roof over their heads, and toys in their room. They love us by giving back every day. As parents, we don't do dishes. The kids do the dishes. They clean up the backyard and pick up the dog poop. They clean their rooms, make their beds, vacuum, dust, wash windows, mow the grass, and wash clothes (all age appropriate). But even a child aged three should begin with simple tasks, moving towards doing the dishes and cleaning the kitchen by age seven.

Chores are, of course, always done with a happy heart, and done without prompting. Kids know what their responsibilities are. We will talk later about this, but we want to raise kids who don't need to be told what is expected. They work hard and do a good job at whatever they do. Chores are how you train them to be successful in the working world, but also how they learn to love you back.

My kids get allowance to teach them how to be responsible with money. But allowance isn't for all their chores. "You do the dishes to help out Mom. You clean the kitchen because you love her." By the time your kids are twelve, the kids should be doing most of the housework.

Don't worry that you are stealing their childhood. From the time he was eight years old, my dad did about four hours of chores a day. At age twelve, he spent the summer cutting timber ten hours a day, six days a week. He cleaned the entire elementary school every night after school. As he always says, it built great character in him. Jason and I did at least an hour of chores every day. Though I hated it, I would not change a thing. I learned more by doing chores than most other things I did as a child. I learned how to love my parents.

Children's chores include cleaning up after themselves. How many moms spend time complaining how their kids never pick up? It's time we stop complaining and we start expecting. They love you when they pick up after themselves, clean up their toys, and put away the games. We don't want to raise lazy spouses who just leave their shoes and belongings all over the house. That is not love.

8. Showing Enthusiasm When You Walk in the Door Is Love
Your kids are expected to be excited to see you. Put this into their hearts. Let them know how it makes you feel when they run up and give you hug; how it makes you feel when they act excited to see you. Nothing is wrong with prompting your kids by saying, "Dad's home. Let's make him feel like he was missed all day." This

is true even for the teenage years. Sitting on the couch and not giving me the time of day when I get home is not an option. (I guarantee it won't be an option when you get married.)

9. Communicating Your Life to Me Is Loving Me
Sharing your day is important. "How was your day?" "Fine." "What did you do?" "Not much."—not acceptable. You love me by sharing your life with me. In this, I am teaching you one of the most important parts of relationships—communication. By the time they get married, sharing their day will be easy. They have been doing it their whole lives. Our kids are expected to love us back by sharing their lives with us, and by listening while we share our lives with them.

10. Love Us in Our Love Language
Finally, we teach them how to love us in our love language. That means taking the time to figure out what that love language is. This takes work, but it's work that pays dividends.

Activity for Review:

Take the following love language test. This will tell you what your love languages are. In each group, rate the sentences 1 to 5 according to what would make you feel most loved by your spouse or children. 5 represents what makes you feel the most loved, 1 the least. You must use each number (1-5) only once in each section.

Group One
A. Your spouse/child says "You did a great job on that. I appreciate it."
B. Your spouse/child unexpectedly does something in or around the house or your room that you appreciate.
C. Your spouse/child bring you home a surprise treat from the store.
D. Your spouse/child invites you on a leisurely walk just to chat.

E. Your spouse/child makes a point to embrace and kiss you before leaving the house.

Group Two
A. Your spouse/child tells you how much he or she appreciates you.
B. Your spouse/child (male) volunteers to do the dishes and encourages you to relax. Your spouse/child (female) volunteers to wash your car and encourages you to relax.
C. Your spouse/child (male) brings you flowers, just because he cares. Your spouse/child (female) brings you home a special food treat from the local bakery.
D. Your spouse/child invites you to sit down and talk about your day.
E. Your spouse/child gives you a hug even when you are just passing by room to room.

Group Three
A. Your spouse/child shares about a recent success you had during a party.
B. Your spouse/child cleans out your car.
C. Your spouse/child surprises you with an unexpected gift.
D. Your spouse/child surprises you with a special afternoon trip.
E. Your spouse holds your hand as you walk through the mall or your child/ parent stands by your side with an arm around your shoulder at a public event.

Group Four
A. Your spouse/child praises you about one of your special qualities
B. Your spouse/child brings you breakfast in bed.
C. Your spouse/child surprises you with a membership to something you always wanted.
D. Your spouse/child plans a special night out for the two of you.
E. Your spouse/child will personally drive you to an event instead of you having to go on the old, crowded bus with the team.

Group Five
A. Your spouse/child tells you how much his or her friends appreciate you.
B. Your spouse/child takes the time to fill out the long, complicated applications that you had hoped to get to this evening.
C. Your spouse/child sends you something special through the mail.
D. Your spouse/child kidnaps you for lunch and takes you to your favorite restaurant.
E. &our spouse/child gives you a massage.

(Transfer your scores from you test questions to the scoring profile on the following page.)

	Encouraging Words	Acts of Service	Gift Giving	Quality Time	Touch
Group 1	A___	B___	C___	D___	E___
Group 2	A___	B___	C___	D___	E___
Group 3	A___	B___	C___	D___	E___
Group 4	A___	B___	C___	D___	E___
Group 5	A___	B___	C___	D___	E___
Totals					

Compare your score with your spouse/child/parent. Write down from the primary to the least of the love languages of each family member.

1. _____

2. _____

3. _____

4. _____

5. _____

Be prepared to share with the class how today lesson has affected relationships at home, church, and work. Discuss areas in which your kids did not love you, and changes you made. What differences in the home did you see?

Your Scenario for Discussion:

You get a call from police station, your thirteen-year-old got caught shoplifting:

Homework for Mom and Dad:

Dads, read chapters 10 & 12 from *More Than a Dad* (chapter 9 is basically this chapter, and 11 does not exist).

Moms, read chapters 10 & 12 from *More Than a Mom*

CHAPTER 7:
Justice, Integrity, Fortitude

Consider the atheist who speaks and writes that, "there are no moral standards. Your ideas of right and wrong are nothing but an expression of your likes and dislikes." But when this person gets lied to, taken advantage of, when someone breaks into his home and steals his stuff, or assaults him, suddenly there is a cry for justice. But I thought there was no moral standard? The person that robbed you was expressing his like to beat the snot out of you.

The world may not be concerned with many of the points of character, but justice is something we all want. It is one of the first things that are important to your kids. "Hey, he has a bigger cookie than mine!" "That's not fair. It is my turn." "He's not sharing." Long before children know what most virtues are, they are crying out for justice.

The problem is, justice is not just about me. It is about all of us. People cry for justice when they are wronged. What a different world it would be if we also cried out when we wronged others.

It is our job as parents to teach our children what justice is and how to apply it to life.

Virtue #4: Justice

Justice means respecting the rights of all persons. It really comes down to the Golden Rule: treat others as we wish to be treated. A parent's job is to put inside our kids an awareness of others and getting them to a place where they are other-minded.

Once again, they learn this not so much from what we say, but from what they see us do. We have to live it to teach it. And while we live it, we put the *whys* into their hearts so they do it as well.

Everything we do should be showing our kids we respect the rights of others. Your family needs to be other-minded. If our baby is crying, we respect the rights of others to enjoy their movie or dinner. We get up and go somewhere that does not infringe on their rights. In public places, we teach our children not to run, to talk with an inside voice, and to allow others to enjoy their time. At the theatre, we teach our children not to be loud and not to touch the chair in front of them. (I am amazed at the number of evil people who bang my chair during the movie. I often times feel bad that I hope they burn in hell. It seems like a wrong thought, but if I were God, I'm 90 percent sure they wouldn't get into heaven.)

When we visit someone's house, my one-year-old is taught to respect others. We don't touch their stuff. We play quietly with the toys we brought. This training, of course, starts at home. You first learn to respect Mom and Dad's things.

At McDonald's, we don't just leave the table a mess for someone else to clean. The Andersons clean up the table and throw away their trash. We demonstrate a love for others for our children to model.

If we borrow someone's possession, we leave it better than we got it. For example, you borrow a vehicle from a friend, even for just a couple of hours. You wash it and fill it up with gas. You make sure you explain why you are doing this to your children. As Andersons, we treat other people's things better than our own.

When we rent a house, Holly does this to a fault. I am paying $3,000 a week for a house and Holly has us mopping floors, vacuuming the whole house, washing sheets, blankets, all these things that I pay the homeowner to do when I leave! If she had her way, I would put a fresh coat of paint on the outside. The house is cleaner than it was when we arrived. Oh, I get mad about it, but I love what it is instilling into the hearts of our children. The same goes for hotels. I need no housekeeping; Holly has the room spotless.

Whenever you use anything owned by someone else, including a big business, company, or individual, your kids are watching you. Do you apply the Golden Rule, or do you say, "Hey, I paid for my meal. You clean it up." Your kids will take that attitude with them into school and jobs – into your home and into their lives.

That brings up another subject. "Can I abuse something based on its outside appearance?" Does the Golden Rule have a loophole? For example, can you litter on a lot if it is trashed? If you borrow your friend's junky car, can you abuse it? Are your actions based on your outside perception of it, or are we held to a higher standard?

I was outside working, and Peyton was playing. He said, "Dad, can you hold my Batman while I get a drink?" He handed me this piece of plastic that had been gnawed on by the dog. It was missing an arm and half a leg. As he walked away, I tossed it aside. Peyton saw this out of the corner of his eye. I could tell immediately that I'd hurt his heart. I quickly grabbed Batman by the half leg and said, "Oops! I dropped it. Peyton, Dad is going to make Batman a special bed." I grabbed some part of a cushion, fit it into a box, put batman in it, took a little piece of a cloth and put it over him for a blanket. Peyton got a huge smile on his face, went inside and got his drink. When he came out, he said, "Dad, you can watch Batman anytime."

How we treat others has nothing to do with the outside appearance. We have to look beyond that and see the person behind it. I don't love the object. I love you. The object has no value to me, but you are priceless, so I will treat the object like it is priceless.

We don't litter even on a trashy lot because that is not other-minded. Someone has to pick up that trash. We teach our kids to look beyond the outside appearance and see that some person owns that lot. We teach our kids that possessions may not be valuable, but other people are.

Example: A friend loans your child his bike. Let's say the family doesn't have much money and the bike is a piece of garbage. Does that give your child the right to treat it like garbage? Absolutely not. We see past the object, and we see the rights of the person. We then treat it like it was our own.

It was an accident? Pay for it.
Being a huge Judge Judy fan (she is so hot), I see so many shows where parents make reasons why their kids don't have to be responsible. A kid throws a firecracker into a car and the vehicle burns to the ground. The parents say if the owner had not left the window open, the car would not have burned. (I would like to use Chapter 10 on the parents.)

One of the greatest lessons of responsibility you can teach your children is retribution. "You broke something that was not yours. Accident or not, you take responsibility for it." Parents, make sure they are the ones paying out of their allowance, even if it means paying you back. Making reasons and excuses for their bad actions may save a few dollars, but those dollars are not worth the cost—raising an adult who can take no responsibility for his actions. The kid breaks a window? What a great lesson your child gets to learn for just a few hundred dollars. That's a bargain!

If they break something in the house, such as a sibling's toy, the same lesson applies. They learn to take responsibility for their actions.

I was with Heath at his gym when he was a gymnast. We backed up was getting ready to pull forward, when a girl and her friend backed into us. I turned my phone on record and got out. The girl apologized, said it was her fault and that she wasn't looking. I got her parents info, and insurance info. When I contacted the parent, the parent said it wasn't her daughter's fault. I sent the mother the recording. The mother said sorry, not her fault. The damage was just a few hundred dollars. This mom missed out on an opportunity to show her daughter the right thing to do. How very sad.

"Kids, look, free money."
It's important that we teach our children not to take what is not ours. That doesn't change in the case of "found money." If we get too much change from the waitress, we say it was a gift from God. We confuse the hearts of our kids for a few bucks. I challenge you to train them that *anytime* we get something we did not pay for; we do the right thing. We demonstrate other mindedness.

I think I will date you, and you, and you.
As your children reach the teenage years, make sure that they follow the Golden Rule in dating. There is nothing wrong with breaking up. Just be sure that you do it in love. Do it the way you would like someone to break up with you. Dating a couple of people at a time is fine, as long as the ones you are dating don't think you are in a boyfriend/girlfriend relationship with them. In a relationship? Don't date others. If you want to date others, then you have to let everyone know, because that is being other-minded. You would hate to be cheated on, so don't cheat.

Dating is practice for marriage. It demonstrates lack of character to toy with people's emotions. It lacks character to cheat. It lacks character to string someone along. You wouldn't like it, so we make sure we don't do it. If your teenager can't learn to be faithful while dating, he will not be faithful when he is married. Being faithful is other-minded.

Authority? No, not today.
Justice includes respect for authority. Consider what's needed for authority to succeed. What do they need? They need respect. Many adults struggle through life because they were never taught how to respect authority, how to submit and how to play by the rules. What rules am I talking about?

> 1 Peter 2:13
> 13 Therefore submit yourselves to every ordinance of man for the Lord's sake, whether to the king as supreme,

> Romans 13:1-2
> 1 Let every soul be subject to the governing authorities. For there is no authority except from God, and the authorities that exist are appointed by God. 2 Therefore whoever resists the authority resists the ordinance of God, and those who resist will bring judgment on themselves.

The Bible says to submit to authority. It does *not* say "submit to authority only when you agree with it." Submit, when it works for you? (We obviously use common sense. If your boss orders you to kill someone, we do not submit to that.)

Suppose your boss gives you a project that shouldn't be yours or asks you to do something that isn't your responsibility. Maybe you don't like your boss, and whatever he says annoys you. You think you know more and could run a better company. These are all normal thoughts for people.

Your boss asks you to do something, you do it. If you don't agree with it, you discuss the issue in a respectful manner, and then whatever he decides, you do. *And you do it with a happy heart.* Respect is a heart issue. If you do what your boss says, but then talk about what an idiot he is to your coworkers, you did not submit. If you come home and complain about your boss in front of your children, you are sabotaging what you are trying to teach them. You say, "Do the dishes," and wonder why they grumble and complain? They will reenact what they see you do every day.

Respect starts with you. You set the stage for their lives. Do you submit only when you agree, or is it the principle that drives your life? Do you demonstrate great character at the workplace and at home?

The ref is an idiot. He lost the game.
If you want to really see the character of parents and kids, go to a kid's sporting event. The ref makes a bad call and parents scream. Kids yell. In the parking lot, everybody is mad and upset at the moron ref.

But the referee is the authority on the field. Whether they are right or wrong does not matter. Character says, "I submit to that call, put a smile on my face, and play as hard as I can." Once again, parents are missing out on a teachable moment. Do you really want to get that mad over a baseball game that (by tomorrow) has no significance at all on any aspect of your life?

Understand your kids can learn so much more from losing or from a referee's bad call than they ever could from winning. They learn how to respect authority, how to smile, take the bad call, and move on in life.

At one particular baseball game, Laken struck out on what was one of the worst calls ever. He was so mad. (On the inside I was too.) He said, "Dad, that wasn't a strike."

I said, "Yes, it was."

"But, Dad, it was way over my head."

"I know, son, but the referee called it a strike, so it was a strike. You have to adjust for the next time you are up to bat. The referee is always right." I taught Laken that the ref is the authority on the field, and Andersons always respect authority.

When a teacher calls, most parents take the child's side. "My kid doesn't listen because the teacher is boring." Her being boring is not an excuse for wrong behavior. "Well, she has the kids doing things that are just stupid." Once again, you are undermining the authority, and you wonder why your kids struggle with authority in the teenage years.

When a kid has a problem with a teacher, parents immediately pull the kid out of the class. You have set an example for his life. When his boss upsets him, he'll quit, because you taught him that lesson. Marriage isn't all it should be, so he moves out because you trained him to quit.

Your children would learn so much more if they learned how to work with and submit to the bad teacher. They will have many difficult people in their lifetimes. Success in life relies partly on their ability to deal with them. (Now, there may be a really bad teacher, and it may be a horrible situation for your child. You tried to work with her or him, and you may have to pull your child out of that class.) But if you find yourself constantly making excuses, then the child is to blame, not the teacher.

Remember, your children will learn far more from submitting to those they don't like than from submitting to those they do like.

Obviously, respect for authority starts at home. I will state it again. First-time obedience with a right heart is so important to their success in life.

Be happy for your brother.
Being happy for others is part of justice. Teach your children to be happy when others succeed and when others get a blessing. "When your brother wins, you need to be happy for him." On birthdays, they should be excited for what their brother or sister is getting.

MAKE SURE you do not buy them a gift on their sibling's birthday. Many parents make the huge mistake of saying, "Well, it is so hard on him. His brother gets all these toys on his birthday, and he gets nothing. So, we get him something nice also."

Parents, *you are feeding the beast of envy*. This child will grow up never satisfied with what he has, always looking to what others get. "How come they got the raise?" "Why did he get a boat?" "How come I never get anything?" Yes, you get a lot. You just can't see it because you are consumed with what you don't get.

Your children need to learn to be happy for their siblings. One kid is going to camp? Don't try and make the other kid's week sound just as fun. No, your children get to be happy when others are blessed. You are raising a child who can live an envy-free life, a child that can be happy when others get blessed and thankful for all they have.

Life is not fair.
Teach your children that life is not fair. Justice and fairness are not the same things. The sooner your children realize that life is not fair, the better. They can stop being concerned with how fair things are and, instead, make things in their life successful.

It is interesting that fair is never other-minded. We never get mad about what others don't have. It is always what we don't have. A child never says, "It is not fair that I can run and jump and there are kids who are in wheelchairs. It is not fair that we have a home, and car, and nice things while there are starving kids in Africa." That kind of fairness is all about self.

We teach our children to be thankful for what they do have. Look to the good in the home. Yes, some kids face situations they don't deserve. Why, I don't know. But I do know that to have a great life, we have to maximize what we have been given.

If you sit around waiting for fair, life will pass you by. Kids and adults consumed with fairness lack the ability to be thankful and to be happy in life. It goes back to being happy when others are blessed. Be happy that your brother got a bigger cookie. Be happy with the cookie you have. Parents, it is not your job to make their lives fair. If you do, they will struggle in the real world where life isn't fair. Look for teachable moments, I almost get excited when something not fair happens. It is an opportunity to train my kids.

Chores
Chores are about being others conscious. I know we talked about this last chapter, but this applies to being other centered as well. According to a study done by researchers in Toronto, Canada, children who do chores show more compassion for their siblings and parents.

What's really interesting are the children who did family type chores (clean the kitchen, sweep the floor, wash the car …) showed more compassion than kids that did self-care responsibilities (make your bed, clean your room, take a bath…)

When children take part in the care of others, it makes them aware of needs that are not their own. As they do for others, it makes them aware of the needs others have.

Now take that idea outside of the home. What a great learning experience it is to have your kids help you donate some time. You go down to the church and help fold bulletins. Take your daughter with you. Feed the hungry. Take your son with you. As they serve, they get a servant's attitude about life.

In these acts, you are teaching your children compassion. Many parents teach sympathy, but that doesn't build character. A person of character has compassion. Sympathy feels bad for you; compassion does something to help you.

Look at an example: A widow comes into the office. She and her children have not eaten in a couple of days. I feel really bad about this. I go back to my office, eat a couple snack packs, and think about how sad that was. Perhaps I make a social media post to express my sadness. I had sympathy for her. I must be a good person.

Compassion would say, "Let me get you something to eat." Compassion *does* something.

Justice means loving myself.
Since we are persons ourselves, justice also includes self-respect, a proper regard for our own rights and dignity. We teach our kids to stand up for themselves, for what is right.

Peyton, our youngest, is a very good boy—respectful and a 'giver' to all who ask. If you were to walk up to him and grab his candy, he would scream. Why? Because inside all of us is a sensor to tell us when someone is not respecting us. Now, if you walked up and asked him for some candy, he would give you some . . . most of the time (he loves his candy).

God put something inside of us to help warn us when we are being a doormat. I am a man with great character. Why is it when someone cuts in front of me in line that I want to beat every square inch of him? In reality, I've only lost a few moments in time. But that little warning device is going off.

We need to train our kids to be sensitive to that and to deal with the situations in life. I refuse to raise a doormat that is walked all over. My kids are taught to love others, but when you infringe on their rights, then they have an obligation to stand up for themselves.

If a bully is pushing them around, well then, I have given them the tools to handle the situation. Most of the time, a bully just needs a punch in the nose. (Yes, I did go from serving people in the food lines to punching in the nose.)

Obviously, I teach my kids how to handle situations, and fighting is a last resort. If someone calls them names, those are just words. You can walk away from words. But if someone is physical with you, now you have the right to stand up for yourself.

This teaches a valid lesson in life. People treat you how you expect to be treated. It teaches them how to put boundaries up in their lives. They won't find themselves as adults if they're being walked all over. My kids say, "Yes, I will love you, but I expect love in return." That is a healthy attitude.

Self Esteem
Parents, in our books, *More Than a Dad/More Than a Mom*, we discuss how to raise your children's self-esteem. Make sure you read this and follow through. How your kids are treated in life is based on how they see themselves. What they think of themselves determines what others think of them. Life will be so much easier if Mom and Dad teach them how to love themselves.

Virtue 5: Integrity

"I hope I shall possess firmness and virtue enough to maintain what I consider the most enviable of all titles, the character of an honest man."
~George Washington

We live in a world where you have to sign a million documents to buy a house. We have to cover every loophole. This is because "giving your word" means nothing. There was once a day when a handshake was worth more than a contract. It was a time where people were concerned with having character. This is how we want our kids to be. We want to raise up men and women of integrity who do what they say and mean what they say.

Integrity means more than just honesty. It involves trustworthiness, objectivity, fair-mindedness, sincerity, thoroughness, keeping our word, and standing up for what we believe. To have integrity is to be consistent (rather than contradictory) in different situations. Integrity is different from honesty, which tells the truth to others. Integrity is telling the truth to yourself.

"The most dangerous of all deception is self-deception. Self-deception enables us to do whatever we wish, even great evil, and find a reason to justify our actions."
~Josh Billings

That is what people who lack integrity do. They justify not doing what is right. They make excuses and reasons for breaking their word. I don't have to follow that part of the Bible because… They are deceived, but even sadder, they are deceived by themselves.

A person of integrity is genuine. What you see is what you get. To live with integrity is to live by the highest standard. A person of integrity doesn't seek to cover up or make excuses for when he fails. This allows him to change, to grow and to become better.

Integrity, like all your children's virtues, starts with you. If you say you will do it, you do everything you can to make sure it happens. Your kids need to see your words and actions line up in all areas of your life. If you tell your kids you will take them to the park on Saturday, it should take an act of God to keep you from going to the park.

If someone is counting on you, you come through. If you give your word, you keep it. If you say you will be somewhere at a certain time, you are there on time.

Dad, I Don't Like Baseball.
If your kids sign up for a sport, they finish the season. So many kids sign up and then quit a few weeks in. That lacks character. The team is counting on you. You gave your word. Now let's do it.

"Sorry, you can't miss the game because your friends are going out to the movies. You gave your word to the team, and they are counting on you."

At age eleven, I agreed to do a paper route with eighty homes expecting delivery every day. After the second day, I decided that the $13 a week was not worth the hours of work. To my surprise, my dad said I had to give them a thirty-day notice. "But, Dad, they will be fine. They can get someone else to do it." (I was making excuses to get out of doing what was right.)
My dad said, "Son, you gave your word, and you will always stick to it." So, I delivered papers for the next thirty miserable days.

By allowing your kids to quit their commitments, you are missing the opportunity to teach them about integrity. Your teenager says she will have a friend over, and then gets an invite from a different friend who has invited her to do something more fun. You tell your daughter, "Sorry. You gave your word."

She will, of course, come up with all the reasons in the world, but her word has to mean something. You will not allow your children to get into the habit of deceiving themselves. (Deep down, she knows what is right. She knows what the Golden Rule says about this.)

Your daughter says yes to one boy for homecoming and then the boy she *really* wanted to go with asks her. "Sorry, dear, you gave your word."

Your kids say they will be home at 5:00. That means they are home by 5:00. Not 5:05. Not 5:01. You said 5:00. "But, Dad, stuff happened." Once again, a lack of integrity looks for excuses and reasons.

My dad always said "If you're on time, your late. Andersons are always early." What if something came up? "Son, you should have left fifteen minutes earlier. Then those unexpected events wouldn't have made you late. You will need to be home right after school for the next week." You are teaching them about being on time for work and even showing up early.

Don't You Trust Me? NO!
Children will lie. That is a fact. Whether they take that into adulthood is up to you. A person of character, when he makes a mistake, makes no excuses and tells the truth.

Every time our kids lie, we need to seize that trainable moment. Let them know that lying tears down the relationship. Relationships are built on trust. If I can't trust what you say, then it limits me on what I can allow you to do.

Obviously, there are different levels of punishment (Chapter 10), but we really want to touch their hearts about lying. If a child has recently lied to me, and a situation needing trust comes up, I am able to say, "See how that last lie keeps me from believing what you are saying now." We explain to our kids, "If we don't have a trusting relationship, don't expect to get your license. Don't expect to get a cell phone. Those things are given to those I trust." It is your job to build trust. Every time you lie, you tear away at that trust.

Integrity in life is so important. Look for moments to train. Look for situations where they gave their word, then train them to do what is right, not what feels right.

Virtue 6: Fortitude

Fortitude goes hand in hand with integrity. Fortitude gets us to do what is right in the face of difficulty. It is about teaching our kids to make the hard choices in life. Most of the time, fortitude is about choosing to look to the good in a problem in life and overcome it. It is about being able to fail without feeling like a failure, learning from our mistakes in life, and becoming better in life.

Fortitude is the inner toughness that enables us to overcome or withstand hardship, defeats, inconvenience, and pain. Courage, resilience, patience, perseverance, endurance, and a healthy self-confidence are all aspects of fortitude.

Teenage suicide has dramatically risen over the last thirty years. I believe that many young people are unprepared to deal with life's disappointments. Their parents have sheltered them from problems, tried to keep discomfort away, and given them a false hope that it is possible to have a life that is problem free. When the problems came into the child's life, as they do in *every* life, the problems seem overwhelming.

Our children need to know that life has problems. A great life has great problems. Holly and I are very successful, and problems are a big part of our life. Without problems, life would be boring. Kids need to realize that problems are not a bad thing if we overcome them and learn from them.

James 1:2-4 says, "Count it all joy when you are faced with problems. They teach you how to deal with life. They help you get to a place where you lack nothing." (Scot paraphrased)

You will either raise kids that ignore problems in their lives or overcome them. They will either sit at the base of the mountains in their lives, or they will climb them. Success in life is contingent upon them being an overcomer. It is your job to teach that to them.

Don't Take All Their Problems Away.
Make sure you aren't trying to shelter your kids from problems. Many parents try and solve all the problems in their kids' lives. They try to remove all the problems. What a huge shock that child has when he gets into the real world! Mom and Dad did not equip him and teach him how to be a problem solver.

Problem Solving is a Skill.

It is important that your children learn the skills needed to solve problems. Yes, your kids need to feel like you are always there when they fall. You are their safety net, but they need to solve their problems.

Many parents ask, "Why math? Why algebra?" They allow their kids to "just get by" in these subjects. No, help them master them. Math is problem solving.

Many parents are against all video games. That is like me being against all books because there are some bad books out there. There are many great problem-solving video games out there; games that teach how to use common sense, reasoning skills, perseverance, and patience to solve them.

Many toys are great problem solvers and help children develop creativity. Look for things to put into your kids' lives to help them solve problems.

Give Your Child the Freedom to Fail.
Yes, we all love to win. As dads, we live vicariously through the victories of our children. "Win one for Dad." Because of this, I wonder if we miss out on how much more our children learn when they lose.

We have to be careful not to put so much pressure on our children that they feel like they can't lose. If they lose, they are *not* letting us down.

Teach your children that if they gave their best effort, losing is fine. In every game, there is a winner and a loser. Failing does not make you a failure. Never trying does. We want our kids to grow up as adults who are not afraid of failure. They know if they don't step out and try, that is failure.

A parent's wrong attitude toward failure can prevent his or her children from stretching themselves to their full potential. A child that thinks his parents will not be pleased with him when he fails will shy away from things he is not great at doing. He will be afraid to try anything new. Their unhealthy attitude toward failing will hold them back.

When the child fails, you need to be just as excited as when he succeeds. Show your child that your love is unconditional. "Win, lose, stink or do great, we love you." Parents, you need to look inside of yourself. Get rid of any junk that gets you mad and upset when they fail. Your child can sense your disappointment. This can hold him back.

Help Them See the Positive
Look to the positive when considering your children's efforts. If it was a game, "Let's talk about the great catch you made," not the three strikeouts. She got her heart broken? "Let's look at what you learned in this." Allow them to figure out the things on which they need to work. To be successful, our children have to learn how to discover weaknesses and how to overcome them. "How could you have been a better boyfriend or girlfriend? What ways can you change?

Reassure Them of Your Love
Oftentimes, a hug and, "I'm so proud of you" is all they need, a reassurance of, "You don't earn my love and affection. It is always there."

Be Present
Your kids need to know that your door is always open, and you are always there to talk. Your goal should not be to direct their lives. Rather, you want an ongoing conversation that leaves them feeling better about life. Yes, this idea is a little tricky, because we *do* want to give them all the answers. But most of the time, the greatest learning comes when they discover the answers on their own.

Being present means you just listen, let them talk, try and hear what their heart is saying. Be positive and try to emphasize the good. Guide them into the solutions without giving the solutions.

Share Your Failures
Many times, talking about your failures and the things you learned as a result can bring a smile to their faces. It is interesting; when we fail, we think we are the only ones ever to go through that. For whatever reason, it is comforting to know that most people go through the same things.

Being Good at Something Takes Work
Teach your children that it takes work to be good at something. If they fail at baseball, get them lessons (or throw the ball around with them in the evening). If they fail at schoolwork, get them tutoring. If they fail in relationships, take them to the bookstore and let them pick out some self-help books.

You must teach your kids how to be successful in life. Later, when the marriage isn't going well, rather than giving up or just sitting back and enduring the pain, they'll have the wisdom to go out and get counseling or read books. They have learned that to be successful isn't an accident or something that happens to lucky people. Success is for all who will learn.

We Don't Give Up
Andersons don't quit in the middle of a problem. We work to solve it. We persevere. We keep trying. Einstein said that every problem has an answer. You just have to keep working to find it. Einstein also said, "I don't think I am smarter than anyone else, I just stick to solving a problem longer than most."

Stress is Not an Option
The Bible says never to worry. Don't be stressed. Scientists have linked stress to over 95 percent of all diseases. Our bodies were not designed for stress. It was great you put so many good

character traits into your kids, but if they worry too much, world is killing them slowly.

Worry and stress are other words for fear. Fear is what keeps us from solving problems.

Fear keeps us from being creative. Fear keeps us from stepping out. We teach our kids how to deal with stress and how to deal with fear. It starts as a child learning to deal with the fear of the dark. I said earlier, "Don't be scared."

"But, Dad, I am."

"Well, don't be. Dad is in the room next door. There is no reason to be scared."

You take the same approach with stress. You don't give in to it. You don't feed that in your children's lives. Teach them how to overcome it. They learn to release that stress, and just do their best. Most adults today would kill to be able to do that.

"Oh, our daughter is so stressed about the test, we are taking her out for ice cream." There's nothing wrong with going out for ice cream, but outside stimulus will never overcome stress. That's avoiding stress. It has to be battled from the inside. Most bad habits come from using outside comforts to deal with inside issues. For example, overeaters will usually say they eat when they are stressed. (Did their parents give them food and treats to help deal with the stress?)

"Honey, don't be stressed."

"But I am."

"Well don't be. Whether you do well or not, as long as you gave your best, it is fine. We are proud of you regardless. You have to remember that and make yourself think that everything is going to be great. Fear will keep you from doing your best." Slowly (and this is a gradual process), they'll train their minds to naturally be stress-free.

"Our son is all stressed out about the game, so we are going to take him out and buy him some things to get his mind off the problem." That *is* the problem. He needs to have his mind on it. He needs to learn how to overcome it. Buying stuff doesn't solve anything.

Look to help your children overcome stress and fear, not live with it. I have found that this doesn't work the first time, or the second, or the third. Do this every time, and then one day, they find themselves. They stop being afraid, they stop being stressed out.

Questions for Review:

1.   What is justice?

2.   Has anyone borrowed something of yours and returned it broken? How did that make you feel?

3.   What are the ten ways we teach fortitude to our children?

Your Scenario for Discussion:

You get a call from your 16-year-old who wrecked the car—it was his/her fault.

This Week at Home:

- What is something that people do that bugs you because it is not other-minded?
- Name something you or your family does, that you recognize is not other-minded.
- Write out a recent experience in either your life or your kids' lives that demonstrated integrity.

Homework for Mom and Dad:

Read chapter 13-14 of *More Than a Dad/More Than a Mom.*

CHAPTER 8:
Positive Attitude, Gratitude, Hard Work, and Humility

Virtue 7: A Positive Attitude

"People are as happy as they make up their minds to be."
~Abraham Lincoln

First, a disclaimer. As we write this next section, please understand our hearts are set on getting truth to you. The Bible says the truth will set you free, but a lie will hold you in bondage. The lie the world has told us about depression holds millions of people outside of the happiness God has for them.

It is important that we get the truth into the hearts of our children. We don't want them growing up thinking that happiness is not for everyone. Some get it and others don't. We don't want them thinking possessions and stuff will give you happiness or that happiness is about what happens to you. No, happiness comes from inside. Happiness comes from choosing to be happy in any circumstance. This next portion is about getting the truth in you so you can pass it on to your kids. I want you to know that every single person who believes what I write next is happy. Those that do not believe it are not. It is a fact.

Choose Happiness
"Rejoice in the Lord always, and again I say rejoice." (Phil. 4:4) Paul said this when he was in prison. During his life, the man was stoned, shipwrecked and persecuted, but his happiness was not

based on circumstances. It was based on choice. "My brethren, count it all joy when you fall into various trials." (James 1:2)

Count it all joy when problems face you. If God says to do it, it means we can. He would never ask you to do something that was impossible. This tells us that being happy, being positive, isn't about our circumstances that happen outside of us but about the choices we make inside of us. We choose whether or not we will be happy. Now, you may not believe it, but that does not change the fact that it is true. You can choose not to believe in gravity, but if you jump off the roof, you still hit the ground.

Chemical Imbalance
"But my doctor says I have a chemical imbalance." Yes, you do. Thoughts create emotions by releasing certain chemicals into your body. If you think negative thoughts, your body releases chemicals to make you feel depressed. If you think happy thoughts, your body releases chemicals to make you feel happy.

Too often, we don't deal with the cause of depression; we cover it up. We try to neutralize the chemical rather than go to the root of the problem. The doctor gives you drugs not to cure depression, but to cover it. You don't feel happy. You don't feel joy and peace. You just feel numb. Mood drugs are Novocain for the emotions. I can't feel the pain of you drilling into my tooth, but in the same sense, my mouth doesn't feel great. The cause is bad thoughts. The effect is the chemical imbalance. We treat the effect.

Let's say as you walk around, you realize that the heel of your foot hurts. Every time you take a step, it's like something is burrowing into your foot. The doctor says, "I have an answer. We will simply numb your foot. There you go, now you don't feel the pain and you can go on with your life." But your foot feels numb all day. It doesn't feel like it should. It's hard to keep your balance because you're numb.

The doctor says, "Well, hopefully one day you will be able to come off the medication." The cause was a rock in my shoe. The effect was pain. Remove the rock and remove the pain.

You have a "rock" in your thoughts. You have been taught to think negatively and see the worst in situations. The Bible says, "Think only on those things that are good, pure, trustworthy..." (Phil. 4:8) *Only means only.* Only doesn't mean some things. It doesn't mean think about good stuff once in while and think about negative stuff the rest of the time. Only means only. God knows that where your thoughts are, your emotions will follow.

I have never met a person who says, "All I think are great thoughts, yet I am still depressed." Some people have all the reasons in the world why they think negative thoughts and why depression is not their fault. Remember, reasons do not change results. No matter how good the reasons, your negative thoughts will not change the results. Look past the reasons and start thinking good thoughts. Take responsibility for your emotions. You cannot fix that for which you do not take responsibility. As long as it is not your fault, you have no control.

Second Corinthians says the battle in life is not out there somewhere, but in your mind, and you have to cast down any thought that is contrary to God's Word. Worry is contrary, fear is contrary, negative thoughts are contrary. "Cast down" means you get mad at those thoughts and get rid of them. You start doing that with every thought, and it isn't long before you are happy.

I say all of this because these are the things we need to teach our children. Outside circumstances do not dictate their happiness. Inside decisions do. Let's look at the keys to instilling this lesson in our children.

Create a Positive Atmosphere at Home.
Anything put in the right environment will be successful. Put it in the wrong environment, and it will fail. You can apply all the

"Train Up a Parent" principles in your kids' lives, but in the wrong environment, you will fail as a parent. It is your job to create the right environment in the home.

Are you moody, down and depressed? Do the kids know to stay away from Dad in the mornings? (He is just not a morning person. He doesn't follow the Bible until after noon.) Is the home down and depressing? Or do you rejoice in the Lord *always*? Is your home full of joy and happiness? Whether your kids hang around home in their teenage years depends on the atmosphere of the home. No one wants to be in a depressing place.

Put a smile on your face in the morning and a smile on your face when you come home from work. "But, Pastor, I don't feel happy." I don't care. You can act happy for the coworkers who will only be in your life for a short while. You can act happy for the waitress who will be out of your life in an hour. Why can't you give the people who will be in your life for the rest of your life the same courtesy?

Create a home that is different from the world; a home where the kids see it is different to be a child of God. We have a happy home, a fun home. It is the parents' responsibility to provide an atmosphere of happiness.

Your kids need to see you attack problems in a positive manner. Setbacks don't stress you out. You remain positive and happy. You demonstrate what will come more easily to them as adults. That attitude is a choice. They see you choose to be happy every day of your life, and for them, it becomes a natural habit.

In the real estate crash of 2010, we lost everything. My oldest son asked me about it recently. I asked if he remembered it. He said, "I remember moving, but that's about all."

I asked, "Did the mood of the home change?"

He said, "No, not at all. Later, I heard what happened in a sermon you gave, but until then, I had no clue." We lost everything, yet the mood of the home was still happy, fun, and God is good.

I want you to know that the atmosphere of the home will determine the quality of relationships you have with your kids. Environment is one of the most important parts of relationship development. You cannot create a great relationship in a bad environment.

Being Unhappy is Not an Option.
I would get up in the morning as a teenager and grumble into the kitchen. Mr. Happy Pants (my dad) would greet me with a big smile. "Good morning, son."

I grumbled, "What's good about it?"

He said, "All right. Leave the kitchen and come back. This time act happy."

"Dad, I'm tired."

"Don't care. Out. And when you come back in, you better have a smile on your face."

There was no moping around the house for weeks. "Oh, he is just depressed. Life is kind of hard." What in the world is hard? Sitting around watching TV, having all your needs met by your parents, and your biggest problem in life is finding something fun to do on Friday night? If this is hard, man, the real world is going to throw you for a loop.

Parents, once again, make excuses for their kids that end up crippling them for life. "Son, life is good. Life is great. Put a smile on your face and get happy. At the very least you will act happy in this house."

Of course, we understand setbacks. The boyfriend broke her heart. The girlfriend dumped him. That stinks, and I know it hurt, but we move on in life. We command our thoughts and get ourselves out of that. We look at the good in life and leave the past where it belongs—in the past.

Sure, there is often a week or two of grace period as they walk through the hurt. But it is very important that they walk through it, not stop and wallow in it. It happened *to* them. It does not become *a part* of them. When my kids went through a break-up, we spent a lot more time with them. We took them out for special one-on-one talking sessions. We helped steer them. This is important. By the time we reached the dating years, we had built a trusting relationship that allowed us to speak into their lives.

Teach Your Kids to See the Good.
Seeing the good in life is a learned habit. Dads, you keep your kids seeing the good in Mom. Mom, keep the kids seeing the good in Dad (even if you are divorced). You keep them seeing the good in the home.

Sure, we may not have all the things the Jones's have, but you do have great parents, parents who love you and do things with you. If your kids focus on the good, then they won't hate the home. If you teach them young, then when they are teenagers, they'll find the good in their parents all by themselves. Show them the good in life, the great things God is doing. Keep them positive about the world in which they live.

I honestly did not know we were super-poor growing up. I just thought everyone else had more. I got a Green Bay Packers trash can for Christmas while my friends got go-carts, and newest video game systems. Yet, I loved my trash can. Teaching your kids to be happy with what they got will be one of the most important lessons they can learn. If we don't do that, they won't be happy with their spouse, with their job, or their life.

Teach Kids to Make Their Own Happiness
Too many parents spend their days trying to keep the kids happy. Kids need to learn how to choose happiness. When outside stimulus is always used to make them happy, they grow up thinking that happiness comes from stuff, and from circumstances. This wrong belief keeps them going from relationship to relationship, job to job, buying thing after thing, looking for happiness in a drug or in alcohol.

That is why room time and playpen time is so important in the younger years. That is why it is so important we don't pick you up every time you cry. We are teaching you how to be happy in any circumstance.

As a young father, I felt that when I was home, I was responsible for every moment to be fun for the kids. This made it hard for me to work around the house. I felt guilty when I did yard work. I felt like I should have been making things fun for the kids. One day I realized that was wrong thinking.

Growing up, my dad did not spend every second with me. He worked on cars, on the house, and paid bills. Sure, we had time together, but a lot of the time I was responsible to make my own day fun. My mom was a stay-at-home mom, but she didn't spend every second with us. Maybe an hour or so, but the rest of the day was up to us.

I think we sabotage our children's ability to be happy when we are the source of their happiness. They need to learn how to be happy without outside stimulus. They need to play outside with a couple of toys, use their imagination, and make a great day all on their own. These kids grow up as adults who are able to take whatever life throws at them and make a great life out of it.

Negative Words are Not Allowed

"I can't. I stink. I'm not smart. I give up. I'm no good." Words are a seed. Every word is planted and will eventually produce. Depression, stress and worry all started with a word spoken.

Parents, make sure you only speak positively in your own life. The children are watching and listening. If you are constantly speaking down, speaking negative, don't be surprised when they do.

Inside of all of us is a recorder. This recorder plays subconsciously all the time. It is this recorder that tells you what you can and can't do. For many people, when a problem comes up, the recording says, "You're not smart enough. You can't do that. Just walk away." These people struggle through life. For others it says, "You can do all things. Yes, you can do that. You are smart. You can be good at anything." These people are successful.

What does your recorder say? What's great about a recorder is, you can change it. You just have to speak the right things over and over until it becomes your new recording.

My mom was told her whole childhood that she was dumb, useless, and nobody liked her. Those were her thoughts in her twenties. At age twenty-four, she could barely read. My mom went out and bought a recorder. She recorded over and over the scriptures that said she could do all things, that she was smart, that she was successful. She played those scriptures every night, all night. Today, she has written dozens of books and speaks all over the world. She changed the recorder in her head.

It is very important that we put the right things on our kids' recorders. I want my kids to hear a voice saying, "You can do it. You are smart. You are good looking. There is nothing you can't accomplish if you put your mind to it."

To do this, we speak only positive over all areas of our kids. We look for times to tell them how smart they are, how handsome they are. "Mom is so lucky to have such a smart boy like you," or "Man, are you good looking." We plant seeds of positive into their hearts all day.

We then make sure that only positive comes out of them. Anytime we hear them say anything negative, we take the time to change that. "No, you are very smart. This is just an area in school at which you have to work harder. Remember that paper you wrote last week? That paper was written by a very smart person. You are very smart. If you want to be good at that, let's work on it."

"I give up."

"Andersons never give up. You can do it. Keep working on it. You are one of the smartest kids I know. If anyone can do it, it is you."

One thing that really helped me in the teen years was my Mom's confession book. At night I would spend ten minutes confessing how smart I was, how successful I was. Parents, teach your kids this. See if you can get them confessing the Word over themselves.

A Side Note: It is important that you teach your kids how to be successful. If they stink at something, teach them the importance of practice. Then the next time they are doing that thing, point out to them how the practice really helped. "Son, see how that extra batting practice helped."

Virtue 8: Gratitude

This virtue goes hand-and-hand with a positive attitude. Gratitude is about being thankful for the things you have. Gratitude, like attitude, is a choice. We choose to be thankful just like we choose to be happy.

Some philosophers claim that gratitude is the secret to a happy life. It reminds us that we all drink from wells we did not dig, meaning, most of the blessings in our lives come from others, come from God, and not from ourselves. We look at life, trying to find the good, trying to find what we can be thankful for, not what we are not getting.

Eddie Rickenbacker, who drifted twenty-one days in a life raft in the Pacific Ocean, was asked, "What did you learn while out on the ocean?"

He said, "If you have all the fresh water you want to drink and all the food you want to eat, you ought never to complain about anything."

We want our kids to grow up thankful for what they have, thankful for what we have provided for them, thankful to God for the life He has given to them. A heart of thankfulness will be a source of their happiness. It will drive them from one blessing to another.

The Bible says to enter into his gates with thanksgiving in your hearts and into His courts with praise. Why? Does thanksgiving change God? Does praise change Him? Understand that thanksgiving, praise, and gratitude do not change God. *They change you.* They change your heart. They change how you see life. You will develop "my glass is half-full" eyes. You'll see life through what God has given you, not out of what you don't have.

Your kids' being thankful does not change you. It changes them. They learn to appreciate all that you do for them, all the hard work, time, and effort that you give into their lives. Teenagers that have been taught to be grateful, love, honor, and respect their parents. They enjoy being around the family.
Kids who were never taught the importance of gratitude, though they were given the world, can't stand their parents. They think their parents never gave them anything. They see the home through the eyes of what they don't have.

As parents, we need to expect a thankful heart. From the time they are nine months old, they are taught to be thankful for all that is in their lives. So, how do you teach gratitude? What lessons should your kids learn?

Be Thankful (Even if You Don't Like It).
Nothing sounds more spoiled than a kid who gets a gift and says, "This isn't what I wanted." That has never happened to us, nor will it. Kids are taught that we are thankful even for the smallest things. Even with things we do not like, we act like it is amazing. Once again, they look beyond the gift, and they see how valuable the person giving the gift is.

Be Thankful for Everything
When kids are young, prompt them to say thank you on nearly all occasions. "Thanks, Mom, for making dinner." "Thanks for the treats." "Thanks for playing with us." "Thanks for taking us to the movie." Slowly, by age five, they begin to do it on their own. Use the jar of character to get them to develop a thankful heart for all in life. No matter how small a blessing is, they are thankful for it. "Thank you" has to become a habit. I hear thank you from my kids many times every day, and they are happy kids. Thankfulness is key to happiness.

Prayer
Prayer at mealtimes and prayer before bed teach gratitude. Teach children to look for the good things God gave them that day. Teach them to be thankful for all the blessings that happen to them during the day, and the importance of thanking God.

Writing Cards
It is a must that the children get each parent a card for holidays. Teach them to write that for which they are thankful. Don't allow your twelve-year-old to fill out the card in two minutes. "I want you to spend some serious time thinking about all the things for which you are thankful."

Point Things Out

Show them things throughout the day that are blessings in your life. Share with your children the great things God did for you that day. Share with them the great things their mom or dad has done or is doing (married or not does not matter). Find the good things. Help them see only the good in the other parent.

I have become very good at this. My kids hear how good God several times every day. If I get an unexpected green light, I say, "Oh, God loves me." If I get Taco Bell, it's because God loves me. I live a life being thankful for everything, and this transfers to my kids. They are the most grateful people I have ever been around. I will simply watch a show with my kids, and as I leave the room, they will all say, "Thanks Dad for watching a show! Best dad in the world!"

If your teenager is having trouble with this, make it a requirement that when they first see you after school, they thank you for a few things they noticed you did for them that day. "Can't come up with any? Go to your room. No music, no TV, until you can come out with some." Do this every day until they can do it every day right away with a sincere heart.

You are raising adults who will find great things in life. They will focus on the good things in their spouse, good things in their job, the good things God has done for them. You are setting them up for a good life.

Virtue 9: Hard Work

"I challenge you to show me one single solitary individual who achieved his or her own personal greatness without lots of hard work."
~John Wooden

Lazy kids turn into lazy adults. Kids with no ambitions turn into adults with no ambitions. It is our job to put the ethics of hard work into our kids.

My dad worked from the time he was eight. His dad would get him up at 5:00, and they would work until dark. His dad instilled the virtue of hard work, and it was this virtue that has carried him into success in every area of his life.

He is so funny; you can't even take your time painting a room with him. He has to work hard and fast, and with excellence. It was a habit his father put into his heart.

We want that same thing put into our kids. When you do your chores, you work hard. You don't work slow and without purpose. If I allow that, then when you do get a job, good luck keeping it. Work smart and look for ways to do the job more efficiently. You never do a job halfway. Excellence is the bare minimum we expect.

"We also expect you to do these things without being told." My kids know their chores. They don't need me to list them. At age eight, you know what your responsibilities are. You are expected to do them every day and do them with excellence.

We are teaching lessons that will last a lifetime. I expect them to work hard in school and do more than is expected. "I don't have to remind you to do your homework. Your boss isn't going to remind you to do your job. It is expected." If you can get that into their hearts at eight years old, it will stick with them for a lifetime.

In sports or activities, to be successful, you have to work hard. This is something we put into their hearts. Every day we have *Become Great at Something Time.* This is thirty minutes spent in practice at being good at whatever they are involved in. Every day we practice fifteen minutes on the piano, and then we go out and practice whatever sport we are playing. We don't prompt them. They know it is expected. We are teaching them that greatness isn't given to you; it is worked for.

What I See, I Do

Have your kids help you, work with you. One, it is a great time of relationship building. Two, you can show them the skills needed to work hard, how to work smart, how to solve problems, and how to save time. Somehow, in the last couple generations, we missed this. Forty years ago, Dad and sons went out and worked on the farm together. Mom and daughters worked all day around the house together. Hard work was handed down generation after generation.

We have reached a hard work gap. I see so many young people today that are just plain lazy. They lack a work ethic and work skills. They can't problem solve. They don't know what hard work is. That will not be the case for our kids. Hard work is a key to them attaining their hopes, dreams, and goals.

Virtue 10: Humility

"If on consideration, one can find no faults on one's own side, then cry for mercy; for this must be a most dangerous delusion."
~C.S. Lewis

"I believe the first test of a truly great man is his humility."
~John Ruskin

"Without humility, we keep all our defects. They are only crusted over with pride, which conceals them from ourselves. Humility enables us to take responsibility for our faults and failings and change those areas in our lives."
~Unknown

"Every virtue turns worthless if pride creeps into it, which happens whenever we glory in our goodness."
~Dietrich von Hildebrand

This final essential virtue can be considered the foundation of the whole moral life. Without humility, we cannot continue to grow in all the other virtues. Humility makes us aware of our imperfections and leads us to try to become better people. Nobody is perfect, and we will never attain perfection in this lifetime. To be successful in life, you have to get up each day saying, "How can I be better today than I was yesterday?" A successful life is one in which the individual spent a lifetime becoming better at all he does.

So, how do we develop humility in our children?

We Don't Brag
Oftentimes, you will hear kids say, "I'm better than you. I'm smarter than you. I'm stronger, faster…" This child, out of a sense of insecurity, has to tell the world that he is the best. You need to nip that right away. Bragging kids don't end up with many friends, if any. And bragging takes them down a road of pride and a false sense of confidence.

Explain to your kids why we don't brag in sports. *We just play the game.* When we win, we are good winners. We don't gloat or rub it in. We are kids with character who know what it feels like to lose, and we follow the Golden Rule. Treat others how you want to be treated.

When you do get around another kid that brags, you have a great teaching opportunity. I say, "See? How does it feel?"

"I hate it," they say.

"Do you want to be around them?" I ask.

"Not at all," they respond.

Make sure they are humble in all activities. They don't raise themselves up by putting others down. Instead, they should want to pull others up to their level and work hard at getting to levels of those above them. (Sports provide a great example. There are plenty of "good" players. The great ones elevate the play of their teammates.)

In all my years of playing racquetball, I have learned that the person who brags about how good they are, usually isn't that good. I have never lost to someone who says they are great at racquetball. I have lost many games to the guys who said, "I'm okay." The ones who are quiet are humble. Those are the ones who will spank you on the court.

Be Good with Correction
Proverbs says a wise man takes correction and learns from it; a fool gets mad at it. We don't want to raise fools, so it is important that we teach our kids to learn from correction.

Don't get mad at it. Don't pout about it. Grow from it. When we get to Chapter 10, we'll talk about discipline. The most important part of discipline is a child who learns from their mistakes so they don't keep making them. A teachable spirit says, "I made a mistake, how can I change? A fool (Biblically speaking) says, "I know. I know. Whatever. It wasn't may fault. There was nothing I could do about it."

After correcting your children, how do they respond? If they are mad and upset for hours, then you should be concerned. If they are upset for a few minutes, come out of it, apologize, let you know what they would do differently, then they are headed in the right direction. The first is unacceptable, and needs to be dealt with right away, even if means visiting Chapter 10 all over, and dealing with that issue.

Admit Mistakes You Make.
This goes for you also. I have made many mistakes as a parent. That's okay. Nobody's perfect. What's not okay is when we can't admit it. "I'm sorry, son, for snapping at you like that. It was unacceptable. I admit my mistake." Many parents rationalize a mistake or beat themselves up with it (I must be a bad parent.) No, great parents make a lot of mistakes, and what makes them great is that they admit it.

It is important that your children learn to admit when they make mistakes; that they get past the reasons and excuses. My dad always said to have an excuse is to admit you're wrong. My son will say, "My dad said the same thing." Excuses are meant to keep you from taking responsibility. That keeps you from changing and keeps you from humility. "Come on, Laken. You know and I know, you could have done something different, and this whole mess could have been avoided. What was it?"

Healthy Self-Esteem is Not Pride.
We want our kids to think highly about themselves, to have a high self-esteem. Don't get this confused with pride. Pride says, "I'm better." Self-esteem says, "I'm as good as." Pride puts others down to make oneself feel better. Self-esteem, out of its self-confidence, is concerned with pulling others up. It is important that we can recognize the differences and that our kids can recognize the differences.

Change is Good
We live change and are an example of change. Your kids should be witnessing your life getting better and better. They see your example and how you are reading books, listening to tapes on how to be more successful in finances, in marriage, in parenting. They see your life get better because you are humble enough to say, "I'm not perfect, but I will be working towards it every day."

This example they will carry with them into their adult lives. They will spend the rest of their lives growing and changing. The amazing thing is that *they start where we leave off.* You have the opportunity to jump start your kids into a great future.

Self-Reflection is Necessary.
The ability to look at yourself and see that changes can be made is called self-reflection. We believe this is what many adults lack. Every bump in the road is someone or something else's fault. In every fight, every circumstance, there is always something we could have done better.

A kid fails a test, and they say, "Well, the teacher is unfair. The teacher is out to get me." No, stop it. I heard one of my boys say this. Nonsense. He needed to study more.

He said, "I studied all last night." I guess that wasn't enough. Guess he should have studied the night before also.

"Dad, that wouldn't have been enough." Okay, we are getting somewhere. I guess you needed to study the night before that as well. He won't win this argument with me; we both know he could have done more. He could have studied more hours, taken better notes, gone in after class, and gotten help. Many parents miss out on a parenting moment like this, because they allow their kids to stop the conversation with an excuse. No, we use this to help them grow into adults who can look at their life, see areas they can be better, and change. The great philosopher Michael Jackson said you have to look into the mirror and make that change.

Questions for Review:

1.   Happiness is a _____?

2.   Thanksgiving and praise changes who?

3.   What are the five ways to teach gratitude?

4.   What virtue is the foundation to a moral life?

5. What are the six things we do to teach humility?

Your Scenario for Discussion:

Your seven-year-old whines about everything.

For Further Discussion:

Were you a parent who felt responsible for the happiness of your children? If so, what changes did you make, and what differences did you see in your children?

Homework for Mom and Dad:

Read chapters 15-16 from *More Than a Dad/More Than a Mom*.

CHAPTER 9:
Pre-discipline Training

A Happier Home

The next few weeks will be so exciting. You will finally start seeing some dramatic changes in the children and the atmosphere of the home. In a very short amount of time, parenting will become enjoyable.

While in the malls this holiday season, I saw what parenting was to most people. It was screaming kids, tantrums on the floor, and toys thrown. I heard variations of "JOHNNY, STOP IT! DON'T TOUCH! COME HERE!" a million times. Parents looked like they were one tantrum away from putting the minivan into the ditch. One "Don't touch that!" from just getting on a bus and leaving town.

That is not God's plan. God's plan is for us to enjoy our kids, whether we are out of the house shopping, or in the house with the family. We should enjoy our children and so should all those around us. The home is happier, you are happier, and most importantly the kids are happier.

Little Johnny is not happy with all the fits and the screaming. He is a miserable child who gets everything he wants but nothing he needs. He will have a very difficult life.

Kids with boundaries and expectations are happy. Walk around the stores with me and my four-year-old. Peyton says, "Mom can I please have a toy?"

"Not today, honey."

"Okay Mom."

That right there freaks out other parents. They want to know what medication he is on and how they can get some. "Is that some sort of hybrid Ritalin? Do they snort it? How in the world did you do that?"

Follow us around and see whose children are happier. Go to the house where doors are being slammed and kids scream at their parents, saying, "No I won't." That is not a happy house, and the kids are not happy.

Now come to our house. Watch as we say, "Laken, please do the dishes. Heath, go pick up the dog poop."

"Mom, come on. It's Saturday."

"No, do it, and do it with a happy heart!"

Off they go, and within a few moments, they are doing their chores and doing them with a happy heart. Nearly every time they say, "Okay Mom. Okay Dad."

This is the home God has waiting for you. I almost never have a child tell me no. The last time was when Peyton was about two years old. We never have a child throw a fit, a tantrum, or scream at us. We never have a child not do what we ask. This is what God has for you. My question is: whose home is happier? The child who gets whatever he or she wants, or the one who has Biblical expectations and is given what they need?

Obedience is the Key
Obedience is the key to a great home. Obedient children are happier, and a lot more fun to be around. You can teach an

obedient child how to be successful. You can instill wisdom in their hearts. You can place Godly character in them. You can't do this in a disobedient child. You can't teach them anything, and you can't put any character in to them.

Unless your children learn Godly obedience, life will be very difficult for them and for you. God said in Colossians 3, "Children be obedient to your parents in ALL THINGS, for this is well-pleasing to the Lord." Not obedient in some things, not just the things they want, but in *all* things. That is the standard. That is the key to raising great kids. To put character into the hearts of your children, they first need to be obedient.

Where Parents Mess Up
This next section is key to the next few chapters. Without this section, the other two chapters are no good. Many parents have tried discipline and claim it does not work. The reason it does not work is because they did not grasp the material of this next section. They keep undermining their own efforts. They cannot get their children to be obedient because they sabotage themselves.

The first part of Colossians says that children must obey their parents. We mess this up because we miss the second part of the verse, "Parents, do not exasperate your children." In other words, don't frustrate them. If you frustrate them, it is hard to get them to obey.

It is important to note that yes, they are frustrated at having to clean up. Having to obey can be frustrating. The chore itself is frustrating, but how you get them to obey is the part that should *not* be frustrating. Let me explain. It turns out there are quite a few ways for parents to frustrate their children. Let's go over all seven of them, one-by-one.

Number 1: Lowering the Standard

I said this in earlier chapters, but it is the number one mistake parents make, so we will say it again. We raise the child to the standard, not lower the standard to the child.

We don't make excuses for their misbehaviors. What we expect from the children is what we will get. When you change the standard, your kids do not know what to expect. When you don't know what to expect, you become frustrated.

It's interesting and amazing how very unhappy children become when they are allowed to wallow in rebellion. They are moody, mad, and upset—throwing fits and tantrums. When you set a standard and announce, "this is the standard," they begin to raise up to that standard and begin to enjoy life because they know what is expected from them each and every day.

They don't have to guess, "I wonder how Mom's going to be today. I wonder if she is moody or Dad's moody. I wonder if I can try to get away with this or get away with that." Instead, they know what is expected.

No one reading this book would like to spend their life on shifting sand. Kids and adults—even your dog—wants to know what is expected.

If you worked a job and never knew what to expect, you'd be frustrated. "Scot, you are in charge of inventory." The next day, "What are you doing? You are supposed to be doing sales! Are you stupid?" The next day, "I thought you were going to take care of inventory?" The boss says to type all reports double-space. You turn in your report, and he says, "What is this junk? It is supposed to be single-spaced." You start work at 9; you come in at 8:30, and the boss screams at you for not being at work at 8. A life of not knowing what is expected is very frustrating!

For some of you reading this, your children are frustrated because they don't know what to expect from *you*. "On some days I can get away with this and on others I can't. On some days, I get yelled and screamed at, and on other days it's no big deal. Some days I get put in a corner."

They don't know what to expect, so they are just gambling. Take a chance; roll the dice, "Dad's in a bad mood and I got yelled at, but tomorrow I will do it again and it's fine, no big deal."

And so, your kids are exasperated. You are wondering why they don't obey. It is because they don't know what to obey. What are the standards?

Inconsistency in parenting—not setting a standard—is exasperating our children, and we begin to see that in all areas of life. In creating this inconsistent world, we have not set them up for a successful adulthood in any area of their lives.

The Standard: When I Speak, You Respond
The standard is this: when I speak to you in a way that requires a response, you respond. I call out, "Laken," Laken says, "Yes Dad?" He doesn't ignore me or answer rudely.

What you expect, you will get. I say, "Please come here." I don't want to hear about "another minute." They come. (They may say, Dad I'm in the middle of something, can I come in a few minutes? We will discuss the importance of this in a moment.)

It's first-time obedience, not second time, not third time. It's first time. That is the expectation.

Number 2: Give Them Time to Change
Parents put bad habits into their children. They allow them to talk back to not do what is asked, and to throw tantrums. Parents allowed the bad habits! Realizing they've caused the problem, they say, "This is the law. You will obey me right away. You will do what I ask."

The child needs some time to get acquainted with the new standards (ones you're going to stick to). They need some time to break the bad habit you put into them. It is very frustrating for them when you say, "Change now!" After all, you may have been inconsistent, and they're wondering if you're going to change your tune.

As I said in earlier chapters, make a game out of the new things you are learning. Give the children a few weeks to get new habits in them. Remind them, in a couple of weeks there is going to be a consequence for not doing what is asked.

Number 3: The Threatening and Repeating Parent
"Johnny, I said come here. Did you hear me?" (He did—everyone in the store heard you.) I said, "Come here, Johnny. Mommy is going to count to three. You better come here right now. (Actually, you said in three, not right now.) "One . . . Johnny you better come here. Two . . . I'm warning you; come here. Two and a half . . . two and three quarters (I wonder if these toddlers are confused in kindergarten when learning how to count. For most of their life counting to three was 1, 2, 2½, 2¾ . . .) Finally, Mom goes to catch Johnny because he takes off running.

Dad says, "Clean up your toys." The child does nothing. "I said clean up." Nothing. Dad gets up, makes a move toward the child, and the child starts cleaning. Dad thinks he has an obedient child, and then wonders why the child is near impossible out in public. Dad wonders why, in the teenage years, the child never listens.

As I said earlier, this can mean life and death. I could tell my two-year-old not to go near the pool, and he wouldn't. Not that I wasn't watching, or tempting fate, because parents make mistakes. The phone rings, the doorbell rings. They forget. I plan for the unthinkable. But I don't have to worry about a child who doesn't listen.

In just the last few months, I've seen four-year-old kids dart away from mom into the parking lot. Thousands of kids a year are run over because of a lack of obedience. We can play in our front yard, and my kids knew not to go into the street. I assure you, each of them only did it once!!!!

I say "Stop," and I guarantee you every one of my children freezes in their tracks. I have needed that command a number of times. It saved both Laken and Peyton's lives. I said, "STOP" and there was no arguing. No "I don't want to." No ignoring me. They stopped, and they are alive today because of it.

The standard is, I call you once. I ask you to do something once. When you do not do that, then we move to consequences. Life is about choices and consequences. Bad consequences keep us from continually making bad choices. The consequence, done in love, is what will bring obedience to the child's life.

When you threaten and repeat, the child does not know what is expected, and when it is expected. Sometimes Mom counts to three. Sometimes Mom wigs out right away. Who knows? This is very frustrating for the child.

When we stop threatening, stop repeating, and set the standard expectation, we clear things up. When I call, you come. It is now the child who determines the consequences. Before, you were the determinant. You decided when you "finally had it up to here" (a quote from most parents). Now, the child knows: If I don't obey, a consequence is coming. If I don't obey, I've *chosen the consequence.*

Some critics will say we are dictators; we are authoritarians. We are far from that. You come into our house, and you will see something quite the opposite. "Laken can you please take out the trash?"

"Sure Mom."

"Heath, can you come here?"

"Coming Mom."

As you will see in later chapters, this is all done in love. Our authority is exercised out of loving hearts that want what is best for the kids. Discipline comes from a deep desire for a happy, healthy child.

The Bible says discipline is love. Don't forsake the discipline of your children because of their tears. Discipline is the only thing that drives the rebellion out of their lives.

And as you will see, discipline is not cold and calloused. Being cold and calloused means frustrating your kids, being inconsistent, threatening, repeating, not instilling character in their lives, and not setting them up for success.

As you will see, we do not come across like the almighty ruler of the house. We take om the context of the situation. Our kids can come to us with a right heart and say, "Mom, I know you asked me to do this, but I was in the middle of this. Can I do it later?" We look into situations. We are always trying to love our kids.

When you have consistent standards, you rarely have to discipline. When we had four boys under the age of 12, I disciplined my kids maybe three times in two years. The older two, Heath and Laken, had some discipline twice in the previous four years. Baylor had maybe two episodes since he was three years old, and Peyton, our four-year-old, had only had one time in a year.

When discipline is done right, done consistently, and done in love, you find your children obeying you nearly all of the time.

Number 4: The Bribing Parent

"All right kids, if you are good in the store; if we don't get kicked out of the restaurant again, Mommy is going to buy you a special treat."

Well done if you are raising your very own Shamu. They do right to get treats. This child grows up to find a very sad reality—the world does not reward you for doing what is expected. This child never moves past level one character. This child can't love because they are always looking at what they get out of it. Everything becomes about them, and what they can get.

When you bribe, you sabotage your parenting. Our children behave at the store because that is what you're supposed to do. They don't throw a fit because that would be wrong. Now, there are times when I get done shopping and I say, "You boys did so amazing. Pick out a treat." They weren't good because of the treat; they got the treat because they were good. They obey because that is the standard, not because of a promised reward. And rewards don't happen every time, because kids are smart, and they'll know. It may be one out-of-ten times. We do not bribe our children, but on an occasion, we can reward them.

There are times when we give our children incentives. We will talk about that in later chapters. Incentives are not for behaviors, but for skills. "Son, if you work on your swimming, and you can swim without floaties, I will take you shopping for a toy." That is not obedient related. Swimming is a skill.

It is funny how we create our own problems. Child number four, Peyton, loves candy. At two years old, he would have traded Mom and Dad in for Snickers bar. Every time I took him to the store, he would ask for candy, and I would say, "Sure." It made him so happy. Then came the day when I said, "No, no candy today." And to my surprise, I had a huge fit to deal with.

We create our own little monsters, and then we wonder, "Where did that come from?" Well, we created it. I will talk about this later, but I want to mention it now. *You cannot give your child a yes if they cannot handle a no.*

Number 5: The Re-negotiator
The movie *The Negotiator* has one scene that makes me physically sick. Kevin Spacey is trying to negotiate with his daughter about being nice to Mom. *He is undermining Mom.* He is trying to be the great dad (while being the worst husband). He is trying to offer to the child things to get her to do right.

This sabotages your hopes of an obedient child. It goes back to lowering the standard. I have to make you an offer to listen to me. I have to give something to you to have you do what I ask. Once again, the child will not do what you ask, because they know if they hold out long enough, they will get a better deal.

What a frustrating process for Mom, Dad, and for the child!
"Little Johnny, pick up your toys. Please pick up your toys. Okay, Mommy is going to come over and help you pick up your toys."

"Time for nap." No, the kid doesn't want a nap. He throws a fit. Mom says, "How about we put a movie on in bed and Mom will lay with you?"

That child has been trained to know that if they fight with you long enough, they will get what they want. You think you are this great parent, and your child listens to you? No, they are getting their way all day long. You wonder why it is such a struggle at the store? You wonder where the fits come from at the nursery?

When they become teenagers, they seem to battle you over everything. Every conflict in the house becomes an argument that ends with slamming doors, and you saying, "Where did this come from?"

I can tell you, it came from their toddler years playing out on a much bigger scale. These kids grow up to be adults who can never do what they should do. At best, they do half. They do the part of the marriage they like, the part of the job they enjoy. The drudgery parts? Forget it. Do we wonder why they are so unsuccessful?

This does not mean that we don't allow our kids to speak into the moment. But we never lower the standard. It is important that the child can surrender to obedience without being given concessions. This means going back to the you don't get a yes, until you can be happy with a no.

Let me explain. There are times my kids speak into the moment I give them out of love. But I only do this when I know I have the freedom to say no, and they are okay with it.

It's bedtime in the summer. No school. The kids say, "Dad, can we have a movie on in bed?"

I say, "No," and they get upset by this. I say, "Just so you know, tomorrow, the answer will also be no. It will be no until I'm certain you can be happy, even when I say no. Once I have said no enough, I can say yes.

I say, "Time to clean up."

"Dad, can we play another five minutes please?"

There are times I say, "Sure." But I will never say, "Sure," if I think they will not be okay with no. You cannot have yes, until you are happy with no.

I may negotiate, but I do not renegotiate. "Time to clean up." They may ask for more time. If I say, "No," the case is then closed. We have no more discussion about it.

Number 6: Context and the Appeal
Nothing is more frustrating than dealing with a legalist. "These are the rules. No matter what, follow them." This is very frustrating to

your children. They need to know that you will look into the situation and make the best decision for them. Your children need a voice that can help you make the best decision.

We don't want to be parents for whom our first decision is law. We want to be parents who make the best decision. Often times, we need the children's input because our first decision can be wrong. We need to be parents of character who can change our decision because it is best for the child.

Suppose you told your son to take the trash out 30 minutes earlier. It is still not done. You wig out, not realizing that Mom had told the son to clean up the family room. Your child did not obey you right away, but his decision had context. Mom asked him to do something else. The heart of the child was not wrong, but if you handle it incorrectly the child will become very frustrated.

Mom says, "Clean your room." The child starts to say something, and you say, "*I said clean your room*. First time obedience." What you didn't know was she'd asked Dad if a friend could drop something off at the house (a real cute guy). She wants to look nice. The child needs to have the ability to say, "Mom, this is happening. Can I do it later?"

In an earlier example I say, "Heath, please take out the trash."

He says, "Dad, I'm in the middle of a show; can I do it in a commercial?" Without that appeal, I could have frustrated my son.

Now, it is very important that the appeal comes with the right heart. If Heath yells, "Dad, I'm watching a show! I'll do it later!" That heart is not right. It is a heart that says, "I will be obedient on my own schedule." This is subtle, and most parents miss it, but the demanding child does not operate from a happy heart. The snappy answer gets the TV turned off immediately.

But a happy heart keeps the authority where it belongs—with you. The righteous heart says, "You're in charge; What would you like me to do?"

Wrong: "Dad, I'm busy; I'll do it later!" Right: "Dad, I'm in the middle of fixing my bike; can I do it later?"

Wrong: "I'll do the dishes after I do my homework." Right: "Can I do the dishes after I do my homework?"

This may seem like a subtle difference, but when it concerns the heart, there is a world of difference! What is amazing is you know the difference, but you never knew you had the right to say, "Wrong heart, child."

There is a difference between your child saying, "I'm going outside to play," and "Mom, can I go outside to play?" There is a difference between your child just getting up from the dinner table and, "Mom, may I be excused?"

Many parents' homes are in turmoil because the kids are in charge. They have taken over and the parents don't even know it. Remember, for the appeal process to work, your kids cannot have a yes until they are happy with a no.

Appeal, in a nutshell, happens when child (with a right heart) gives you new information. The new information helps me make a better decision, one that is not cold and calloused, one that is not frustrating to the child.

Rules of the Appeal
1.   *You can only have a yes if you can handle a no.* Children who cannot handle a no, do not get the right of the appeal. There are times when I want the trash out. Guests are coming in five minutes, and Heath says, "Dad, I'm in the middle of a show; can I do it when a commercial is on?" Sorry, guests are coming. "Okay, Dad."

The reason Heath would normally get a yes from me is because I know he is okay with a no.

2. *The appeal can only be made to the parent giving the instruction.* Going to the other parent is undermining the first parent's authority. "Dad, Mom wants me to do the dishes, but a cute guy is coming over." So, Dad gets to be the hero and Mom the mean person? Absolutely not!

3. *An appeal can only be made with a right heart.* The second the child does not have a right heart, so they lose the appeal. "I'll clean my room later. I'm working on my bike." I explain that had he asked correctly, he'd have won the appeal. The consequence of a wrong heart is losing the right to that appeal. Thus, you teach them to come with a right heart.

4. *We do not renegotiate!* You appeal once, and if I say no, the answer is no. We do not keep hashing it out. I tell Heath guests are coming. Take out the trash. He doesn't and keeps saying, "Please, Dad, come on, five minutes." That is the same as not being able to take a no. So, guess what? You do not get a yes.

5. *We do not appeal everything.* If your kids start making silly appeals to everything, you get to appeal nothing.

6. *Make sure you are fair and willing to change when you make a bad decision.* When your children feel like you have their best interests in mind, that you are fair, they are more willing to take a no. The realize you have a good reason.

7. *Instruct in Love.* Suppose, men, that you are fixing something in the garage. You are deep into it, and your wife comes out and tells you it's time for dinner. You say, "Give me a minute while I finish up." She insists. "You know what, I don't care if it is time for Jesus to come back, I am finishing this up." Women, suppose that you are deep in a movie, and your husband comes in turns off the TV and says, "Time to go." Actually, it is time to fight!

My point is this: It is very frustrating to be in the middle of something and be expected to quit right away. It is exasperating, and so it is for children.

We all like a little warning. "Honey, dinner will be ready in five minutes." This gives you time to emotionally prepare and finish what you need to do. "Honey, we are leaving in fifteen minutes." We provide each other a courtesy warning. We need to share the same level of courtesy to our children.

The kids have been working on a Lego castle for the last hour, and you come in and say, "clean up." The kids protest. You cut them off, because you are the parent, and you will have first time obedience. "No, clean it up now." That is exasperating to your children. You wonder why the kids threw a fit? Guess what? You would have thrown the same fit, even though you are 35 years old.

You tell your kid, "Time to take out the trash" and he explains you're in the middle of a show. You say, "First time obedience; you take it out right now."

That is not love, and you are frustrating your kids.

We should try to give our children a five or ten-minute warning. "Kids, we will start cleaning up in ten minutes. Wrap up the game." Kids are able to emotionally prepare for that.

"Heath, take out the trash."

"Dad, I'm in the middle of a show, can I wait until a commercial?"

"Okay, take it out during the next commercial."

Parents, try to give your children a warning:
"Kids, we will be getting out of the pool in five minutes."
"Kids, we will be leaving in 10 minutes."
"Kids, we will be cleaning up in 5 minutes."

Many parents create their own fits. They create their own tantrums. You say to your four-year-old, "Let's get out of the pool right now!" You wonder why the fit occurred. Guess what, you would throw a fit too!

The Bible says, "Do not provoke your children to wrath!!!!" That is exactly what you are doing.

Now it doesn't mean we always give a warning. There are times when I look at the time, and we have to go right then. I am very apologetic to the kids because I made the mistake. "I'm so sorry kids, Dad messed up. We have to go right now. Please put the game up." My kids do fine with this because 99.9 percent of the time, I give them at least a five-minute warning.

Questions for Review

1. What does Colossians warn parents against?

2. List out the seven ways we frustrate our children and give a brief explanation of what each is.

      1.

      2.

      3.

      4.

      5.

      6.

      7.

Your Scenario for Discussion

Your 7th grader comes home with an F in Math, saying it's the teacher's fault. The teacher keeps losing assignments and besides, the teacher hates them.

This Week at Home

Dads and Moms, read chapters 17-18 from *More Than a Dad/More Than a Mom*

CHAPTER 10:
Discipline: Don't Be a Fool - Part I

Discipline will bring wisdom to your children, but a child left to himself brings shame to his mother.
Proverbs 29:15

Disclaimer: In order to write the next three chapters, we read a dozen books on discipline. Honestly, we could not find one or come up with one that is as good as *Growing Kids God's Way*. I believe they wrote that to near perfection. Because of this, this chapter and the next two chapters are based on all the principles they have in their book.

What is Discipline?
Before we discuss discipline, we need to first understand what discipline is.

Number 1
The Bible says discipline is love, meaning its purpose is to love our children. "I love you so much, that I have to bring this consequence into your life." Oftentimes, discipline is harder on us than them. We want so much for them to be happy and have great lives. That makes it very hard to bring consequences into their lives. But the Bible says, "Do not forsake the discipline of your children because of their tears." I love you so much, that I have to do something I hate and that is to bring a consequence into your life.

Number 2

Discipline is a means to change the direction a child is headed. In that meaning, we find our goal. *Our goal is to change our child's direction.* Suppose your child is hanging out with the wrong crowd. What do we do as parents to change that area of their lives?

Your son is getting bad grades. Okay, what consequences in life will bring change? Your three-year-old throws tantrums, how do we bring change?

I want you always to remember that discipline is about changing direction. It is about changing the heart, changing what is going on inside of your child.

We will be giving you very specific methods to do this for all situations in life, but you have to go back to the goal. The goal is changing direction. That dictates how we discipline each of our very different children. A spanking may not change your daughter's direction on a particular issue as efficiently as taking away the phone, internet, and all communication with her friends. Grounding your twelve-year-old boy from the same infraction may have no effect on him whatsoever, so another means of discipline is needed. Once again, write this on your heart. Discipline is about change. What do we need to do as parents to change their direction?

Most parents think of discipline as spanking. The truth is, if you follow the principles laid out in these chapters, spanking will be something you rarely have to do (if ever). I have not spanked my two youngest kids. They are now twenty and fifteen. I don't know if the older kids sat them down and explained, or maybe we just got better as parents.

Discipline Flow Chart

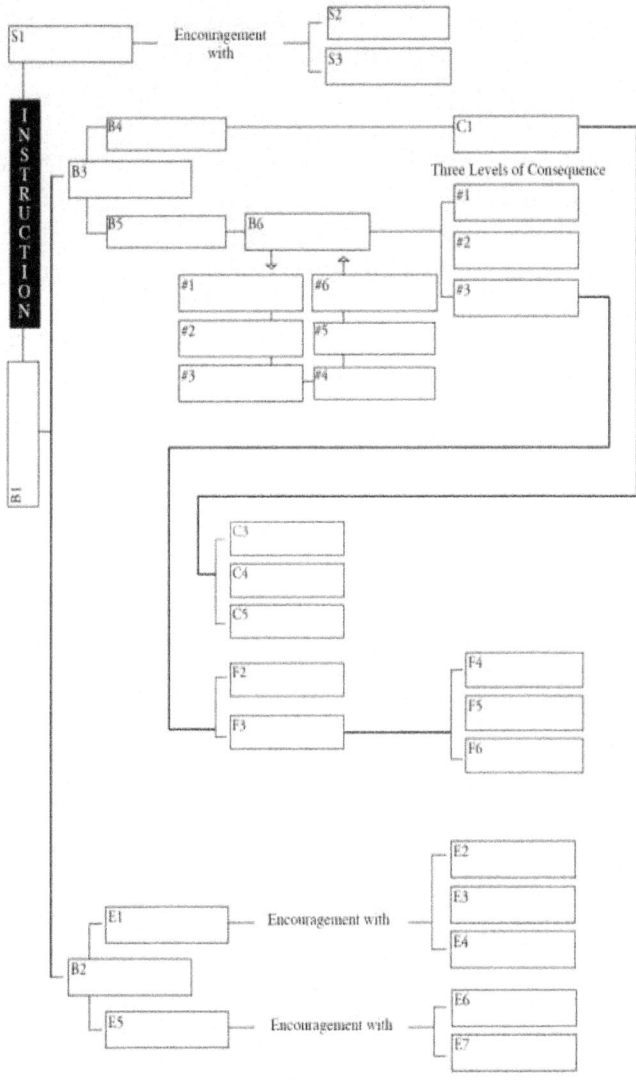

When I watch my granddaughter, I find that my experience and wisdom helps me to navigate discipline without ever spanking her. The benefit you have in reading this now (rather than ten years ago) is our learned wisdom. Our revision of the book is most apparent in our increased understanding of discipline. Our goal is to help you raise great kids and never have to spank them—just like our youngest two.

Parents who consistently follow the model we provide end up doing far less discipline. You'll experience less screaming, yelling, and frustration. Watch other parents at the stores pulling their hair out and going off on the child. Now watch us enjoy our lives with our children.

The Heart a Parent Must Have for Life
Your three-year-old and you are out at a park and a drug dealer comes and tries to drag him off. What do you do?

Whatever it takes, right?

You'd say, "you will only get that child over my dead body." Suppose the same parent has a 16-year-old who is out of control, doing drugs. Would that parent then say, "What can I do? I'll just give it to God."

Why wasn't that your response with your three-year-old? "All right, drug dealer, what will be will be. I'll pray on this."

For the rest of your life, your attitude has to be, *I will do whatever it takes, give whatever I have, lay down my own life, even give up my own life, if it will save yours.*

The Bible says there is no greater act of love than to give up one's life for another. Some guy tries to take your three-year-old daughter? You would die before that happened. Now, your 16-year-old daughter is in love with a 20-year-old bum. "Well, we will just pray. We tried grounding her and it didn't work. We said not to hang with him, and she did anyway."

No.

You have to have the same attitude—"you will get my daughter over my dead body." My daughter will sleep in my room. I will put an alarm on the house so she can't sneak out, I will take time off from work and go to school with her. I'll attend all her classes, hanging out with her and her friends. I will be around 24/7, until she can make right choices.

I lay down my life for you. I love you so much, I am even willing to give up the love you have for me (because I know you are going to hate me right now). That is all right. One day, when you grow up and become engaged to the man God has for you, you will sit me down and say, "Thank you, Dad, for loving me so much that you wouldn't let me throw my life away."

I have seen things go the other way—parents who just let their daughter do what she wanted. Now the girl is in her 30s, and she resents her parents for allowing her to do that. "Why would you allow me to ruin a portion of my life?" she asks.

At age 15, I was hanging out with the wrong crowd. I figured, what can Dad do? Nothing.

Wrong. He took everything away. He said he was my *only* friend. He said, "until you pick good friends, you get no friends."

I was so mad at him back then. As for that school friend of mine, he's been in jail for nearly 20 years now. "Thanks, Dad, for loving me so much, you wouldn't let me ruin my life."

Come on, parents! Tell your children. "I wouldn't let someone take you at three, I guarantee you no one will take you at 15. I will do whatever it takes. I'll lay my life down, and I'll give it up if I have to. But you will not ruin your life, and I am here to make sure of it!"

At the end of this chapter, you will find a flow chart. This amazing flow chart will give you the basics for every situation that you come across with your children.

Walk through the flow chart. This is how you handle things. It is an amazing thing. Put it in your heart. Memorize it. (You don't want to go to the chart every time the child does something wrong. If you're out somewhere, they'll say, "Johnny when we get home, Dad is going to look up what to do!")

Don't Be a Fool

"Foolishness is bound up in the heart of a child; The rod of correction will drive it far from him." Proverbs 22:15 (NKJV)

Children are born with foolishness. We didn't train them to be foolish. I didn't sit down and show my two-year-old how not to share. I didn't teach them how to throw a proper fit in a store. I didn't instruct them in the ways of meanness and self-centeredness. They came with that built in.

It is our job to train that foolishness out of their hearts. If you don't do that, you will raise a child that lacks character and struggles in all areas of life. You will raise a fool

Many of you out there probably know a fool or two. You probably work with a fool. You see them on a daily basis. There are fools in the world, and you can't have a relationship with them. They are unable to have any success in life. Mom and Dad didn't train the heart. If you train up a child in the way they should go, they will not depart from it. It is our job to drive the foolishness far from them.

The Bible says, "All the issues of life flow out of the heart." It is our job to drive the foolishness out of their hearts. If I don't, then by the time they are teenagers, they will do a lot of foolish things. They will act like fools.

Be Consistent
As we go through the flow chart, realize again, consistency is one of the most important factors. Either you do the flow chart all the time, or you might as well not do it all. If you are inconsistent, your child's behavior will be very inconsistent. As you learned in the last chapter, inconsistency only frustrates your kids.

Never Parent Out of Guilt or Fear
Do not allow guilt to hold you back, or fear losing their love. *Discipline is love.* If you allow their tears to hold you back from what they need, your child's future will greatly suffer. But more importantly, your relationship will suffer as well. You will be to blame for their bad life and bad choices because you didn't discipline them. *You* allowed the guilt and fear to hold you back from giving your child what they needed. *You* have to be willing to lay it all down for them, even their love. Remember this Chapter's opening scripture—don't allow your child's tears to keep you from discipline.

Parent for the Future
On that same note, if you allow guilt and fear to get you, you are parenting for the moment. You wouldn't handle your money in the moment—you'd look ahead. You wouldn't skip repairs on your car to go play—the problem might get worse. You wouldn't skip a mortgage payment in order to take a vacation. You have to parent for the future. What I do today will echo throughout my child's life. I may not be a fun Dad today, but I will trade that for being a great Dad tomorrow.

The Flow Chart
In your flow chart we are going to talk about two different kinds of discipline. There is discipline with encouragement and discipline

with correction. We are going to talk about the encouragement side first.

To raise great kids, we can't just focus on the negative. We want to be parents who spend most of our time elevating the good.

Take a glance at your flow chart. Write skills in S-1. In B-1, write in behaviors.

We have separate section for skills and behaviors because not everything in life is a question of morality. Certain things are morally neutral. For example, learning how to swim is not moral. It is a skill. Learning not to splash your brother in the eye while swimming is a behavior. That's a moral choice.

Making your bed is a skill. However, once you know how, the decision to make your bed before school is a behavior. It is very important that you know the difference because each is treated differently.

Throwing a baseball is a skill. Not throwing a baseball at your brother's head is a behavior.

In the skill area, we want to teach our children how to be self-motivated, how to practice, how to be good at things in their lives. Whatever our kids do, we want them to learn how to do it to the best of their ability.

"Whatever you do, work at it with all your heart as working for the Lord, not for men." Colossians 3:23 (NIV).

If they want to go out for baseball, that's fine. But they need to practice and get better at it. Trying out for baseball is a skill, but quitting is a behavior. You signed up? Stick it out throughout the season. Kids need this habit and thought process in their hearts. Later in life, when they stink at marriage, they'll work on the marriage. We don't quit. We don't give up.

Side Note: We believe it is very important to have your kids in sports and/or music. We keep our kids busy throughout the year. There are plenty of benefits, including first-hand experience with the benefits of hard work, team play, sportsmanship, dedication, and inward drive. It also helps kids with their confidence.

To be honest at the beginning of parenting I thought all kids should be in sports, Holly believed all kids should be in music. After twenty-seven years of parenting five kids, we believe all kids should be in both music and sports.

Music is a priceless skill that transfers to so many other areas. Sports keep kids active, healthy. A busy teenager is a teenager that can't get into trouble—they're just too busy.

Savannah just said to me last night, "Dad, I have no free time." I smiled and said "Good." She has tennis lessons every week, she does cheer five nights a week, and she has piano and voice lessons each week. She leads a band at church, this requires one practice night, and one performance night. She has all honors classes. Even if she wanted to get high, she wouldn't have the time.

Anderson's do sports until they graduate high school. For music, piano is a sure thing. From what I've heard, it is a great steppingstone to any other instrument.

When our kids were younger, they had a routine. When they get home from school, the homework was done first. Sports practice for a half hour, and then music for a half hour.

Our immediate goal is to motivate our children to excel at all they do, but our ultimate goal in parenting is to develop children that will self-motivate. I don't want to raise up a child that is okay with being average in life. I want to raise up a child that wants to be excellent in everything he or she does.

Verbal Praise
In S-2, write in verbal praise. When it comes to skills, kids are looking for that praise. Why else would your three-year-old be so excited when he colored inside the lines? He's looking for that praise. Don't miss opportunities to praise, and to build up your kids. Try not to let a day go by where you don't notice something good they did and miss praising them.

One of the things we like to do is point them back to the practice. "Laken, you really hit that ball this week. How many nights did you practice?"

"Man, you nailed that piano song. All that practice paid off."

Point them back to the factor that brought them success in that area.

You also want to call to attention how they feel. What did it feel like to play the song all the way through? What did it feel like to hit the ball the first time? What kind of emotion did you have?

Pointing this out will help them draw a conclusion about what changed to get them where they are at now. When we call attention to their feelings, we help them remind themselves, which is very powerful. We all remember when we did something well and what it took to get there (in many cases, practice and time).

The Praise of All Praises
One of the best types of praise is the unexpected or the unprompted praise. The praise that says, "I watched you when you didn't know I was watching. I watched because you're important to me." You didn't have to show me your picture. I came over and said, "Wow!"

Every day, look for the opportunity to praise. Your praise is the engine that will fuel the success they have in their talents.

It is one thing to praise the kids in the home, but when you praise them in front of others, that is the greatest praise. I start talking about Heath to Grandpa or to one of my friends, he perks up and gets that little shy smile of happiness. *We all love to be praised in front of others.* Don't miss the chance to do it for your children. "Man! Peyton has really been working out at the gym. Check out the guns on that boy!" My nineteen old just smiles, but that simple comment to grandpa makes his heart soar.

Goals and Incentives
In S-3, write in goals and incentives. Don't get this confused with behavior here. We are talking skills and talents. I wanted Baylor to learn to ride his bike. "Okay, son. When you can, ride your bike on your own. I'll work with you for me-and-you time." The goal is to help him with the skill.

"Laken, for every homerun you hit this season, Dad will give you $10." Those are incentives for skills. I would not say, "Baylor I will take you out for ice cream if you don't ride your bike in the street." That is trying to buy behavior with a bribe. Not the same thing.

"Laken, if you don't throw a tantrum during the baseball game, Dad will give you $10." Laken needs to do the right thing because it is right. We don't bribe our children for behaviors, but we can reward them in their skills and talents.

Set reasonable and attainable goals. If the goals are unreasonable (if, for example, your insecurities driving them to be the best player on the team, and they're not physically gifted enough), the goals will actually discourage them from doing their best. And that phrase is the key. *Our kids do not have to be the best at what they do, but they need to do the best they can do.* Your son may not have the natural born gift to hit the ball as far as some kids, and that is fine. I ask that my children try their hardest, which includes practicing on their own.

Behaviors

In B-1, write in behaviors. Behaviors deal with the heart, and it is with these that we must be most concerned. Great, your son can hit the ball farther than anyone else, but if he's into cocaine when he's 16, what good will that do? Awesome that your daughter plays the piano better than anyone her age, but she ran off with a loser at age 15. Skills are important, but the heart is what matters. The heart will dictate the success or failure of their lives.

Encouragement
In B-2, write in encouragement. Even with behaviors, it is a key to our parenting that we look for areas in their behavior to encourage them. Look for great things they do and give them that pat on the back. I often see more change in my kids from a pat on the back than I do from a "don't do that." I would rather say, "I'm proud of you for doing that" than "That was wrong. Stop doing that."

Pre-Activity
In E-1, write in pre-activity. You would be surprised how you can actually dictate the behavior of your child before an activity takes place. This is one of the most powerful parts of this outline. We remind our children what the standards are before we get to the activity.

There are three different types of pre-activity encouragements. All are so powerful. I've done things with my three-year-old with and without the pre-activity encouragement. I highly recommend using the *with*. The difference is night and day.

For example, when your ten-year-old gets to the church, sees their friends, and takes off running, you have to shout," Don't run in the church." It's better if, on the way, say "Kids? Do we run in the church?" By doing so, I bring the behavior to forefront of their minds. Lead me not into temptation? I think this does exactly that.

Verbal Reminders
In E-2, write in verbal reminders. A verbal reminder is just that—we remind the children of the expected behavior before we get to

the activity. "Peyton, when we get to Grandma's, don't forget to say please and thank you. Make sure you give Grandma and Grandpa a hug before you run off and play."

Questions
In E-3, write in questions. Questions are my favorite. For example, on the way somewhere, we ask the kids to tell us what appropriate behavior will be for where we are going.

There is something powerful about getting your children to think about appropriate behaviors instead of simply feeding them the answers. By answering your questions, you are getting their input and their commitment. The responsibility for doing right is theirs. This by far is one of most important things you can do.

So, we are going to Grandma's, I say "Peyton, we are going to Grandma's house. How do we act at Grandma's?"

He says, "No running in the house. Don't touch Grandma's nice things. Say please …"

This is so effective, especially with younger children. When they are able to verbalize behaviors themselves, it helps them to take ownership in how they act, and ultimately, how they will live their lives.

For whatever reason, kids in their younger years tend to forget a lot of that stuff, and if you remind them before you get there, it will help them remember. "I don't run, don't touch, don't throw fits, and don't ask for candy." You will be surprised at the difference in your two- and three-year-old just from this simple activity.

Peyton, Don't Pee on Floor Story
Peyton was two at the time of this story. We were going to the store, and I said, "All right, kids, we are going to Wal-Mart. How do we act in the store?"

The kids said, "We don't run, we don't touch stuff unless we ask, and we stay with you." Then Peyton added, "And we don't pee on the floor."

I said, "Thank you so much, Peyton. We almost forgot that one!"

Positive Words
In E-4, write in positive words. Parents, we tend to get into the habit of saying everything from a negative point of view. This brings an air of negativity into the home. Instead, we should be trying to say most things from a positive point of view.

We get into the habit of always saying, "Don't do this. Don't say that. Knock it off." You would be surprised at how many things you can say in a positive manner rather than a negative one.

For example, instead of saying, "Don't spill your drink," you could say, "Be careful with your drink." There are ways that we can say things and still be positive. Tomorrow, pay attention to what you say to your kids. Find out if you are positive or negative. If your words are negative, then it is something you need to change right away. That negativity will bring a down, depressed atmosphere into the home.

Notice that I said, "find out if you are positive or negative." You may think of yourself as a positive person and be surprised to discover that your words present a different picture.

Post-Activity
In E-5, write in post-activity. It is interesting that when we do something and are encouraged afterwards, we tend to want to do it again. We, like—even *need*—encouragement in our adult lives.

Kids are the same way. They will tend to share more if encouraged when they share. They will give more when they are encouraged after they give.

This is a powerful force that many parents miss. We are so caught up in what the kids don't do, we forget to encourage them for the great things they do. After a while they ask themselves, "Why do it?"

For example, we might have noticed the two kids who didn't make their beds, never said anything to the one kid who made the bed and cleaned the room. We see the kid running in the store, but we failed to praise the kid walking in the store.

There is something about positive reinforcement. Even at 53, when my parents come over and say, "You did a really good job," it matters to me. How much more powerful is it for your children! You're able to come up to them and reinforce what they have done, giving positive encouragement in their lives.

Praise
In E-6, write in praise. "Kids, Dad is so proud of you. Did you see all the other kids in the restaurant? That kid screaming in the corner? I am so lucky to have such great kids. Peyton, thank you for sitting in your chair and coloring. Laken, thanks for taking Peyton to the bathroom. That was a huge help."

Come on parents, you will see their faces light up. Remember, our goal is for them to do good. Why in the world would we not praise them when they do?

Touch is so Powerful
Do not forget the power in touch. God gave us the need for human touch. Touch can say things that words cannot. Try a little hand on their shoulder and say, "You know what you did for your bother that was so nice. You shared, and I am so proud of you." Add the touch and you will be amazed at the power it has.

Yes, we will talk about correction, but if possible, I would rather train and teach my children with encouragement.

Reward

In E-7, write in reward. There is nothing wrong with a tangible reward once in a while when your kids have done something right. But understand that it is not to stimulate behavior. It is to reinforce it. They are not good because they are going to get a reward; they are good and, surprise, here is a reward.

Once again, I am not good because I will get a reward. I am good, and sometimes my parents reward me. See, they don't act good to get something. Instead, we sometimes surprise them with a reward to reinforce their choice to do the right thing.

I may get done shopping, and the kids were amazing and so patient, though it took way too long. I say, "Guys, get a toy. I am so proud of my great kids. Thank you for being the best boys ever."

Bribing a child may get you a result in the moment, but the bribes can never end. They do things on the outside, not from the inside. Giving a child reward every time they are good sets them up for a hard life. But a surprise reward helps reinforce the actions of the heart. I reward you because out of your heart came right behavior.

Questions for Review:

1. Explain what discipline is.

2. What must parents be willing to do for their children for the rest of their lives?

3. What is the difference between a skill and a behavior?

4.   When praising a skill, what should you try to point the child back to?

5.   What does Peyton say you should not do at Wal-Mart?

Your Scenario for Discussion:

Your child says they don't learn anything in their junior high church class. He says they learn more in the big service with you. "All they do in class is play games." (Obviously, this is untrue. The church is teaching the Bible and probably playing a lot of fun games and activities.)

Your child is playing on your emotions, knowing exactly what to say. But you wouldn't pull your kid out of math class because they say they don't learn much.

This is a social problem. Like all of us, your child may feel insecure. What is the best thing for them? Go to their class and learn to make friends (LOL; I answered this one.) But you can still explain how you would handle this.

Homework for Mom & Dad:

Read chapter 19-20 from *More Than a Dad/More Than a Mom*.

CHAPTER 11:
Discipline: Don't Be a Fool - Part 2

Discipline your son and he shall give you rest. He will give delight to your soul.
~Proverbs 29:17

We continue with the amazing flow chart. No more guessing, hoping you are disciplining right. Parents can now confidently move forward with the correction of their children.

Remember that discipline without love is abuse. Discipline is love. It comes from wanting what is best for our children. Not what they *want*, but what they *need*.

Discipline is about changing their direction. We see where they are headed, and we know it is not good. We love them so much that we will not allow them to ruin their lives. We will give everything up, even the love they have for us to save their futures. They will be mad at you now, but in days to come they will thank you for loving them so much that you would not allow them to ruin their lives.

Last Chapter, we talked about the positive side of discipline—disciplining with encouragement. I believe that disciplining with encouragement should become our most often-used tool. But if we did not use the correction side, we wouldn't get to encourage much. This chapter is about correction.

Warning: If you haven't been spanking, don't start today. It is important that you wait until next chapter when we explain how to spank. Spanking done right can change the heart of a child. Done wrong, it can scar that same heart.

The Game
This week, use the game. Let the kids know the standards when they don't do them. Let them know that next week everything changes. And get out your flow chart.

Correction
In B-3, write in correction. Correction is just that, correcting your child. To correct something, you make it right. The child is going down the wrong path. You get them on the right path. The child is making a mistake. You help them correct that mistake.

The Most Important Question
When it comes to correction, the most important question to ask yourself is, *what was the intent of the heart?* Was it an accident or rebellion? The Biblical words are *childishness* and *foolishness*. Childishness is an accident. Foolishness is doing what they know was wrong.

Was it something that they knew they shouldn't do or was it something that they accidentally did? It's important that you ask yourself the question because it determines our course of action. If you get this wrong, you will fail at correcting your child.

Childishness and Foolishness
In B-4, write childishness. In B-5, write foolishness. Once again, childishness is an accident. Foolishness is rebellion (doing something they know is wrong).

For example, Baylor is walking with his milk to the table, and he spills it. That would be an accident. Correction would follow the childishness area of the flow chart.

I tell Baylor as he is pouring the milk to make sure he uses two hands while carrying the milk to the table. Baylor elects to use one hand and spills the milk. That would be rebellion. It would follow the foolishness side of the flow-chart. Same result (spilled milk) but different heart.

Another example. Laken and Heath are playing catch outside, and the ball flies through our window. That was an accident and would be considered childishness.

But if I have told the kids not to play catch by the back window, and they elect to do so anyway? The broken window is rebellion and is foolishness.

In both examples, the result is the same, but in each example, my means of correction changes.

When a child willfully does not do what you ask and goes against a known rule, that is foolishness or rebellion. Rebellion requires a certain correction.

Conversely, there are times when kids just make a mistake. That is childishness and requires a whole different means of correction.

Understand that disciplining childishness the same way as foolishness (or foolishness like childishness) will undermine the entire correction process, and you will not see good results. If you treat childishness like foolishness, your kids will grow up resenting you. If you treat foolishness like childishness, your children will grow up foolish! Let's first deal with childishness or the accidents of our children.

Warning
In C-1, write in warning. The first thing we do with childishness is give them a warning. For example, Baylor is carrying his milk and he spills it. I let Baylor know he needs to be more careful with his milk. He needs to use two hands. Baylor also has to clean up the milk himself. That teaches him to be responsible for his own mistakes. You make a mess? You clean it up.

So many moms miss this trainable moment. They just clean it up themselves because it will be done right and done more quickly. But doing so misses the chance to teach and train your child.

Cleaning up a mess isn't fun. It teaches that child that, yes, mistakes happen, but when you make a mistake, you are responsible for cleaning it up. This alone may help Baylor be more careful next time with his drink.

Parents understand a mistake has been made, but we use the mistake as an opportunity to give a warning and teach a lesson about responsibility.

Another example—the kids are playing video games. Dad yells down and says, "Kids let's go get some ice cream." Laken gets so excited he forgets to put the video games away.
That's not rebellion; it's getting caught up in the moment.

The following day when I wake him up, I say, "Laken, you left the video game out last night, so I had to clean it up." (Remember from earlier chapters—I always give him the "why.") I explain responsibility. Yes, we can get caught up in the moment, but it is important that we are still responsible.

Your children need warnings, especially when childishness is involved. Your daughter's bike left on the lawn? You say, "I know you were excited. You had to tell Mom something, and you ran in the house, but someone could steal it. Tomorrow, you're going to want to make sure that you put your bike away."

Related Consequences
In C-2, write in related consequences. Some mistakes get the warning, but they also move on to the related-consequences stage. These accidents require a consequence, and with these consequences they need to be logical. They need to make sense. They need to somehow be related to the mistake.

Like Baylor's spilt milk, there was a consequence that made sense. Had I said, "You have to clean up the entire kitchen after dinner," that wouldn't make sense.

The purpose of the consequence is to keep kids from making the same mistake over and over. Do you ever see an adult keep making the same mistakes? This comes from parents who did not train them how to overcome mistakes in their lives.

Property
In C-3, write in property. Let's go back to Laken and the video games. A week later, Laken is playing games again. I've given him a warning, but he leaves the game out again. Yes, it was an accident again, but obviously the warning did not change his direction. Somewhere around three times (unless there is a long span where they were cleaning up their game), I need to take correction to the next level. I say, "Laken you left the games out again. This is the third time in a week. No games tonight." The consequence was related to the accident, and it was enough to hopefully teach him responsibility.

It's our job to train responsibility into our kids. You see, most parents just keep warning the kids. I told you to put that away when you are done (day after day after day.) The parents then wonder why the teenager can't hold a job, can't get good grades, forgets things, or is irresponsible with the car. The reason is simple: you didn't correct the child's irresponsibility!

Suppose Laken continues his mistake. The next night he forgets again, then the next night again. There is a point where I then have to assume foolishness. Yes, I understand you keep forgetting, but it is foolish that you do. Here is a new set of consequences that will help remind you. (We will get to those later.)

Privilege

In C-4, write in privilege. I had told Peyton, who was four years old at the time, that he could bring his cupcake into the TV room and eat it. I told him to be very careful and eat it over the plate. When Peyton finished his cupcake, it looked like a pack of rabid wolves had attacked it. Cupcake crumbs everywhere. It was hurricane cupcake.

Was that rebellion? No, just childishness. He didn't mean to make mess. He wasn't throwing the cupcake around, but because he wasn't careful with it or maybe he wasn't old enough for it, I had to take the privilege away. For the near future, he needed to eat his cupcake at the table. In addition, he needed to do damage control over hurricane cupcake.

Personal Responsibility
In C-5, write in personal responsibility. Your child makes a mistake, and it affects other people or damages their property. Who is responsible? Most parents say, "No one. Hey, it was an accident." It sure was, but why should I pay for your child's accident?

I love Judge Judy – one of my favorite shows. Watching this show and seeing parents trying to keep their kids from responsibility is very, very sad. A kid is playing with firecrackers, and it burns up a guy's car. The parents say, "It is not our fault. It was an accident!" Kids are playing baseball and a kid hits the ball through a window. Parents say, "It is not our fault. You can't direct a baseball. Why should we pay?"

Really, you think the person who was just minding their own business should pay for your child's mistake?

Parents, do we love money so much that we are willing to trade in our children's character for it? Are you willing to make up stupid reasons to get your kids out of responsibility? Having your child save up and pay $150 for that window is a lesson they will never forget. It will sit in their heart, helping to guide them as adults.

Your kids are screwing around at somebody's house, and they break the other kid's toy. It was an accident. I understand it was an accident. Your kid did not mean to break the toy, but your kid should be responsible to pay for that toy.

Now, maybe they don't have the money right then, but you can go down to the store and buy the toy and then take it out of the kids allowance or give them extra chores. The child learns a priceless lesson about responsibility. You cannot buy that type of lesson for $20! Why would you fight it?

I can remember Jason and I were golfing in the backyard, and that's not the wisest thing to do when your backyard is only twenty feet by ten feet. We actually had been hitting for a long time. Most of the balls went over the fence, or who knows where, when we put one right through Mom's window. Mom was sitting there praying and reading the Bible, and she thought must have thought, "Jesus is coming back."

Here I am in the fourth grade, and Jason and I had to pay for that window. It was $40.00. Doesn't seem like a lot until you realize I made only $2 a week. Guess what, I did not repeat my "accident." Whenever we played an outside game with a ball, I found myself looking around and seeing if it was safe to do so. That lesson made me become a more responsible person.

Make sure your kids know that if they break something, even something of yours, they are responsible to pay for it. It teaches them to be responsible, but more importantly, to be other-minded. They should look past their own world and put themselves in other people's places. If Mom and Dad accidentally broke my Nintendo, I would hope they buy me a new one, even if it was an accident.

Rebellion
We covered the accident side of children's behavior. Now, let's go after the rebellious side. Write in section B-5 "foolishness."

"Foolishness is bound up in the heart of a child."
~Proverbs 22:15

Read Proverbs and see where a fool's life is headed. If parents do not drive foolishness out of a child's heart, that child will grow up to be a fool. A fool that brings heartache to his mother and sorrow to his father. A fool is unsuccessful in everything in life. It is our job to get that rebellion out of their lives before it destroys them.

Listen closely to this—it's huge. Foolishness basically means deceptiveness, deceit, and rebellion. The scriptures describe a fool as one who reached adulthood whose parents never trained the foolishness out of them.

I don't want to have a fool for a child, but there are many fools out in the world whose parents did not get that foolishness out of their hearts when they were children. Our job is to do just that.

In a nutshell, foolishness is not doing what they know is right! But let's make a list anyway: disobeying, talking back, not willing to accept correction, willful defiance, fits, tantrums, pouting, whining, the evil eye (when your child gives you that look, parents, you better correct that one quick), pretending not to hear, talking disrespectfully, using a wrong tone of voice with you, talking rudely to you. I could list out thousands of them. I think deep down we all know. That is rebellion.

I want to go back to Laken forgetting to put the games away. There comes a time when something crosses over from mistake to rebellion. Laken is rebelling against correction. He is not taking on the responsibility for learning from his mistakes. You keep telling your child to make their bed. They keep forgetting. There comes a point where it is now rebellion. I told you yesterday, and the day before, and you still can't remember. You are rebelling against the correction I have given you. Now we will be giving you something that will help you remember!

Warning to Parents
Each of your kids probably are very different. One kid may act out; one may not. One may challenge you; the other may not. Just because one child does not challenge you on the outside, does not mean they are not challenging you on the inside. The inside is much more serious in many ways.

Let me explain. Most parents deal with the kid who is outwardly rebellious because the rebellion is easy to identify. They tend to overlook the other child who is rebellious on the inside. Come the teen years, you have parents saying, "I have no idea what happened. He was such a great kid and then all of a sudden?"

Actually, it wasn't, all of a sudden. It had been going on since the child was two. Rebellious foolishness has now worked its way from the inside to the outside.

When a child throws a fit, you deal with it. But the child that gives you the evil eye while they do what you ask gets off. Yes, the child did what you asked, but did so with a heart of rebellion.

You correct a child, and the child pouts and does not talk to you for a few days. Most parents are like, "Well, what do you do?" I will tell you what you do. You treat it like rebellion. The Bible says, "Wise is the man who can be corrected." My parents would say, "Go to your room, and you have ten minutes to get out of the attitude and come out here and be happy, Scot."

What if the child is acting like they did not hear you? "Oh, sorry, I didn't hear you." You know, and I know, and the kid knows, they heard you. This is rebellion and needs to be dealt with accordingly.

"Oh Dad, sorry I forgot." Well, that makes three times this week. Let's give you something to help you remember.

What about the mumbling under their breath? Parents, this better make you mad—your children should never mumble while walking away from you!

We see the child who is outwardly defying, who is outwardly disobeying us, and we're able to deal with those. What we don't do is see the children who are passively rebelling. If not dealt with, passive rebellion will develop into active foolishness when they get into high school.

It goes back to the standard. *We want their hearts more than the action.* Great, your son did what you asked, but he gave you the evil eye the entire time. Honestly, it would have been better if he just told you no. If you don't deal with it, then later it will come back and haunt you.

Awesome, she cleaned the room when you asked, but she went in and slammed the door on her way to do it. Once again, it is the heart with which you are concerned. We do things with a happy heart. I don't want to raise a grown-up adult that is still pouting and whining. I want to train that out of my children.

The Foolish Filter
In B-6, write in foolish filter. The foolish filter helps you decide where to go with the next step.

Consider the following:
1. Age of child
2. Frequency of behavior
3. Context of the situation
4. Overall character of child
5. Punishment that fits the crime
6. Punishment is in reasonable period

These are six things that we need to ask ourselves when the child does something foolish.

Number 1: Age of Child
You're probably going to treat your two-year-old (who you told an hour ago not to touch the freshly painted wall) a lot different than you treat your ten-year-old. You have to take that difference into consideration.

Number 2: Frequency of the Offense.
Your child tells a lie, but it is the first one you can remember for a long time. You treat that differently from the child who has lied four times this week.

Number 3: Context of the Moment
Your eight-year-old is embarrassed and lies about wetting the bed. That is entirely different from the child who lied about hitting his sister. The first is more childishness, while the second is foolish. We never want to go back to where the letter of the law outweighs justice.

You're at a party, and you just asked your son not to run in the house, but he joined in the fun. There is still going to be a consequence, but it's probably not going to be the same consequence if I say, "Don't run in the house" and, by himself, he chooses to do so. Two different situations. Both require discipline, but at different levels.

Number 4: Overall Character of the Child
You have a great kid that always listens, but this once, he gets in trouble at school. I deal with that totally differently from the child that is in trouble in school all the time.

Lately, your child has had a real attitude problem. The child mouths off to Mom. That is totally different from the child who is always respectful, always speaks in the right manner, and talks back to Mom once. I have to look into the situation and say, "Where did that come from?" Maybe a bad day at school? What is going on? I have to consider this when I decide on consequences.

Peyton never throws a fit, but one night when I asked him to go to bed, he threw a major fit. I have to look into the moment. I come to find out that Mom said he could stay up and watch SpongeBob before bed, and Dad did not know. The fit is unacceptable, but, for tonight, I probably will just explain that to him, and walk him through the right way to handle it. If Peyton was throwing a fit every night, I would deal with that entirely different.

Number 5: Punishment that Fits the Crime
Make sure the consequences fit the crime. There are so many times, especially with young parents, they either over-punish or they under-punish. They don't realize that when they punish a child, they put a value on what the child did. They put a value on the bad behavior.

If your son kicks your daughter, punches her, and you say, "Go sit on your bed for ten minutes," what you did is put the value for kicking and hitting his sister—just ten minutes on his bed. Later in the day, he leaves some toys out, and Mom sends him to his bed for ten minutes. What you are saying is that hitting your sister is no worse than leaving out toys.

Later that day, the kids are chasing each other, and they trip over a vase and break it. Mom wigs out – it was her special vase. Both kids get a spanking. So accidentally breaking a vase is worse than hitting my sister. The vase is more valuable to mom than my sister.

You put a price on what they did—and don't imagine that the kids didn't notice. It's important that we ask ourselves, "Does the punishment fit the crime?" We don't want to over-punish, and we also don't want to under-punish. Once again, the purpose of punishment is to correct, to bring change. When you over-punish, you frustrate your child. When you under-punish, no correction will take place.

You don't have to decide on a punishment right away. Most of the time, especially for those that are new to this, it is okay to say, "Go to your room." Think things through for yourself, and then explain the punishment to the child.

It's important that any punishment come from a desire to better your child, not out of your emotions. Yes, they dented the car, and it makes you mad, but *things* are replaceable. Your child is not. Calm down. Now, what punishment fits the crime? More importantly, what punishment will change direction?

Number 6: Punishment Happens in a Reasonable Time Frame.
Make sure the punishment happens in a reasonable period. I know people who've said, "My daughter did something a week ago, and she's gonna get a spanking." Why hasn't she gotten it yet? "Well, her dad hates to spank so we are waiting on him." That is just the stupidest thing I've ever heard.

We want the consequences to come in a reasonable fashion. You sit back, take a look at the situation, and say "This is what we are doing, and when we get home, this is what's going to happen."

If I were a child, I would want to get the bad thing over with. No one wants a spanking hanging overhead.

As you will see, discipline provides punishment, then restoration. The longer it takes to punish, the longer until we can restore the relationship. When punishment is not timely, the child lives in guilt and is very frustrated. The restoration allows the child to release that guilt and move back into that great relationship with Mom or Dad.

There is nothing wrong with Mom saying, "When Dad gets home, you're going to be sorry." Or when you're at a store, saying, "When we get home, you will get a spanking." (I love when my parents used to say, "When we get home, remind me to spank you." Sure Dad; let me write that in my day- planner.)

The Three Consequences
Once the offense has been through the filter, we will go to one of the three consequences.

Level 1: Verbal Warning (Write in)
So, your kid does something foolish. You take it through the filter and decide a warning is needed.

For example, Baylor is nine and is being very well-behaved in a restaurant. We are sitting down to have a nice family meal, and out of nowhere, Baylor screams, "I AM NOT A BAYLORINA!"

I run this through the filter and decide this requires a warning. Baylor has never done this before. So, I tell Baylor listen as I explain to him how rude he'd been to the people here. If the other boys are saying something mean, just quietly let us know, and we will handle it.

The behavior never happened again. (It is important to note that if something foolish keeps happening, the method you are using is not working. You need to go on to the other levels of consequences.) Remember, the goal of correction is to change direction. If a verbal warning changes direction, great. If not, then we need to go to number two. If twenty minutes later, Baylor does it again, well, the warning didn't do the trick.

Level 2: Warning plus Removal (Write in)
Jesus prayed, "Lead me not into temptation," or Father keep temptation away from me. Parents, this is our job. It is not fair to keep a child in a situation they cannot handle, and then punish them for not handling it.

Let's go back to Baylor and the restaurant. After a second infraction, I would simply move him next to me. I would tell him that he can't handle the responsibility of sitting next to somebody else's kids, for example. Those are the kids teasing him. Rather than let him sit there building up the frustration until he screams out again and gets in major trouble, I simply move him to another spot. Or maybe I would go sit over by the kids. (Maybe I would whisper something really scary into the little brats' ears. Just kidding. Kind of.) I remove Baylor from the temptation of evil.

Here's another example. Laken is playing a video game. The game is getting the better of him. He starts to get mad. I say, "Son, it is just a game. Don't let it upset you." A few moments go by, and he lets out a semi-silent yell of frustration, and you can tell it is taking everything in him not to throw the controller. I say, "Laken, pause the game for five minutes. Get yourself under control." When the five minutes are up, I explain to him, "If he can't control his emotions, we will be turning the game off for the day."

I saw where this was headed. I gave him a warning, and then I removed him from the temptation. I also taught him a lesson of controlling his emotions – learning to step back when he is frustrated.

Suppose that you can tell that the kids are getting on each other's nerves. You know they are getting close to a big fight. "Okay, kids, you lost the privilege of playing with each other for 20 minutes." (It is a privilege to play with your best friend or your sibling—always put that in their hearts.) Twenty minutes later, talk to them about being best friends and about being kind. You will be surprised at the difference that 20 minutes make.

You removed the temptation. You also taught them an important relationship truth. Sometimes we get on each other's nerves. Sometimes it is good to take a 20-minute break from your spouse before the big fight comes. Go for a drive, a walk, and come back and enjoy each other.

One more example. There are a group of kids who, whenever your child is around, get into trouble. I have a great idea for your child. He doesn't get to hang out with them. See, we fixed that problem very easily. Oh, and if you do hang out with them, then we simply move to level three, which we will discuss next week.

"The companion of fools, becomes a fool! "
~Proverbs 13:20

Questions for Review

1. Define and explain what correction is.

2. What is the difference between childishness and foolishness?

3. Make a list of rebellious behaviors.

4. List out the six things in your foolish filter, and briefly describe each.

Your Scenario for Discussion:

Your sixth grader gets in a fight at school. Do one for both they started the fight, and the other person started the fight.

Homework for Mom and Dad

Finish up *More Than a Dad/More Than a Mom*.

CHAPTER 12:
No Pain No Gain

Remember that the goal of discipline is simply to change direction. If I can change direction without a spanking, then that is the route I will take. Spanking is that last thing. For some kids, taking away their phone is way worse than a spanking. So, we take the phone. We find the kid's kryptonite and we use it to change their direction. When discipline is done right, you almost never spank. Peyton and Savvy have never had a real spanking, just the little taps at three-years-olds.

Before we get into this, I really want to make the point that spanking is our last resort—when direction just isn't changing. I'm older now, with a granddaughter, and I see myself finding inventive ways to change Olive's direction. The goal is to change direction, if I can do that without a spanking then that is the correct course of action.

Who Doesn't Love a Good Spanking
This chapter is very special to me, not because I'm a sicko who likes a good spanking, but because every spanking I have ever had in my life was a significant experience. Every spanking brought change to my life. Good change; right change. I was headed in a wrong direction, and the spanking put me back on the right path. It got me out of my bad attitude and allowed my relationship with my parents to continue growing.

I can remember every one of the six spankings that I got. I am thankful for each spanking today. That is what I want your children to have with you. I want them to get to my age and say, "You know what? Those spankings that I got were good. Those spankings that

I got actually brought my parents and I closer together. Those spankings changed my direction."

The Goal
The goal is to use correction done in love, to bring your kids back to what is right. It is using pain to brand God's principles onto their hearts. Pain to bring change of direction.

Consequences are a Part of Life
Consequences are a principle set up by God to help us make good choices. Consequences are there to help us learn not to hurt ourselves, others, and to do what is right. You touch a hot stove, it burns. The pain is there to keep us from destroying our bodies.

We do not want to be parents who remove consequences from our kids' lives. Those kids see very little success as adults. We want to imitate our Father God, who doesn't remove consequences, but instead, walks us through them.

Think about it. If God would take away all of the consequences, you won't have to work, you can just stay home, and when you need money you pray, "God send me some money." I can treat people however I want, because all I have to do is pray God's favor on me, and I am going to have favor.
But that's not the case, is it?

God doesn't take away all of our consequences. When we make bad decisions, He'll help us get through it, but there are consequences. If you treat your spouse like garbage for twenty years, I don't care how much you pray, she's going to leave you. God cannot make her love you because she has a free will.

If you show up for work late every day, and you don't work hard, and you just sit at your desk and do nothing, you can pray that God makes your boss give you a raise all you want, but God is not going to take away the consequences.

It's important that our children know that the decisions they make have consequences. When they become seventeen, eighteen, and nineteen years old, they will understand that if they make good decisions, they get good consequences, and if they make bad decisions, they get bad consequences.

There are many young adults today destroying their lives. They are on self-destruct. They keep touching the hot stove of life. Their parents never taught them at an early age the importance of making right choices and the importance of having Godly character. They have all their excuses and reasons as to why life stinks Bottom line? They make wrong choices day after day.

Our job as parents is to train our children to make good choices. I want Laken, Heath, Baylor, Peyton, and Savannah to make awesome decisions and choices. How do I do that? In their growing-up stage I continue to give them consequences or allow natural consequences to come into their lives.

"Son, what you said to your brother wasn't a good choice. Here are the consequences." The consequence is teaching them how to have great relationships. How, later in life, to walk in love. To learn to say right things. I am helping them learn how to make right decisions in their relationships.

Consequences
Going through the flow chart, we have gone all the way down to consequence.

On level three, write in consequence. Remember that our goal is to help our children to make wise choices and decisions and to realize there are going to be consequences for bad decisions in life.

Pain is the result of bad decisions. Touch a hot stove, get burned. You don't touch it again. You yell at mom, get a spanking, and you don't yell at mom again. Pain helps you control the urge to touch the hot stove. Pain will help your children control their emotions, control their actions, and control how they respond.

Pain is an external stimulus that controls the internal heart, so that in time, they become self-governed from the inside out. It was pain that got them to follow Biblical principles in the beginning, but later, as they see the blessings of following a life of character, they then choose right from the character that is in their heart.

As a parent, you have trained your child in the right way to go, and THEY CANNOT DEPART FROM IT.

Pain
In F1, write in pain. Pain comes in one of two ways.

The first is *natural consequences* (written in F2). Sometimes foolishness provides its own consequence. I say, "Peyton, don't touch the fire on the candle." He sneaks over, touches it and gets burned. While he is crying, I don't give him a spanking for touching it. He already got his consequence. I comfort him in his consequence, letting him know that when Dad asks him to do something, there is a reason.

I don't gloat. "Got you! Glad you got burned, you little fool!" I'm not happy he's in pain. But I'm happy that he learned something. He learned his lesson, got his consequence, and I know we have changed his direction.

I say to Laken, "Don't run around the pool." Laken runs around the pool, slips on the wet concrete, falls down and scrapes himself. Now do I walk over and pick him up and put him over my knee for being foolish and spank him? No! He's already gotten hurt. Yes, he was in rebellion, but he's already received his consequence. He is in pain, and he's crying. He's hurt, and he realizes now that maybe Dad knows what he is talking about. His pain is a *natural consequence*. Once again, hug, love him, and remind him of why we listen to Dad. This supports that dad has his best interest at heart.

I hate to ever see my kids get hurt, but I have to say that the natural consequences provide the strongest learning tool. In the child's heart, they associate listening to Mom and Dad and not getting hurt. As teenagers now, Dad says, "Don't do drugs." Inside, the child has a habit of listening to Dad and Mom. This is because, as a kid, when I didn't listen, there was pain. Dad said I would get hurt running, and I did. Dad says I will get hurt if I do drugs, and I bet I will.

Laken was playing his Game Boy, and once again the game was frustrating him. I saw him hit the device. I said, "Laken, if you hit it, you will break it." Well, the next day the Game Boy no longer worked. Now, the other boys have their Game Boy to play with, but he doesn't. He now has to save up for another one. The broken device is a natural consequence.

When he could afford another, he treated it like a little princess. Pain brought self-control to his life. Many parents would run out and buy the child another one to ease the pain. That child learns nothing, and no change comes to the child's life.

In F3, write in *structural consequences*. Rebellion sometimes does not produce pain. When it does not come naturally, it needs to be produced through structured consequences.

Telling Mom, "NO!" brought no immediate pain. There were no natural consequences. Without consequences, the child would continue to say no. Put another way—why not touch the hot stove if it does not burn? Pain will quickly help the three-year-old gain the self-control not to tell Mom "No."

There are Three Types of Structural Consequences
In F4, write in logical consequences. Once again, the event in question goes through the filter, and you determine that a logical consequence is needed. Remember, the goal is to change direction. Gender and age all play a huge part in what the consequence is.

For example, your twelve-year-old daughter was caught watching a television show she shouldn't watch. This, after you caught her and warned her just days earlier. A logical consequence might be to take away the TV for a day.

If she does it again, that consequence obviously does not work. Let's do three days. If that doesn't work, you have to take the consequence to the next level. Now she loses her cell phone, having friends over, going out, and TV for a week. Problem solved. Do not forget the purpose of pain—to change direction. If direction does not change, you must raise the level of pain.

A Note about Human Nature
If the reward for misbehavior is greater than the consequence, then most people (children especially) will take the risk. If hanging out with the wrong friends is a lot of fun, and the consequence is that I lose TV for a few days, well compared to hanging out with the friends, that is no big deal. But if you take away everything in their lives until they pick right friends, the consequence is much bigger than the reward, and the behavior changes. To change a child's behavior, the consequence must be greater than the reward.

If throwing a fit in the store means we leave the store, and the child didn't want to be there anyway, the fit will happen again. The reward is greater than the consequence. But if we leave the store, get home and get a spanking, the consequences are much greater than the reward. Behavior will change.

Your sixteen-year-old gets a speeding ticket. (We don't go to court and try to find a loophole, and we definitely do not pay the fine for them). The teenager pays for his own ticket, wastes a day at driving school. If it happens again, well we might repeat the same. A third ticket? Well, now I look at taking the car away. I have to raise the pain level. You lose the car for a week. That does not mean we drive him to school. Sorry, that is what the bus system is for. I'm sorry your friends can't pick you up. Amazing thing, the behavior changes.

You tell your 16-year-old to be home at 11 on Friday night, and they get home at 11:15. No phone call, just late. "But Dad, it is just 15 minutes, and traffic was bad."

"Sorry excuses just mean you are wrong. You should have planned to be home at 10:30 to give you some slack in case there was traffic. I love you, so next time you need to be in at 10. If you are late again, we will change it to 9." Amazing thing, they'll be in at 9:45, behavior changed.

For younger kids, logical consequences are usually not used. We usually go to F4 and F6. Grounding your five-year-old usually will not do any good. The consequence has to change direction, and that means it has to be age and gender appropriate.
For a 12-year-old boy, like I once was, a spanking changes direction real quick. But for a 12-year-old girl, taking her phone away may change her direction a whole lot faster.

A long time ago, we had some parents come to us about a reoccurring problem they had with their seven-year-old daughter. I asked them what the girl's consequences were, and they said they took her phone privileges away for a month. I almost blurted out, "That is the stupidest thing I have ever heard!" It's not a logical consequence to take a seven-year-old's phone or to tell your three-year-old they can't spend the night at someone's house.

Logical Means it Makes Sense
I am sure that every person reading this book has been grounded for life. A year's consequence lacks logic. It's too long and you will never hold them to it.

Now, you may say you are grounded until you get your grades up. That gives them a goal, something to work toward, a reason to change. Grounding for a year is too far in the future. Why change now? You may ground your son from the car until he becomes more responsible. That gives him something to work toward.

In most cases a week should be fine, a month at the most. If that doesn't work, then you raise the level of pain, not necessarily the length of pain. Honestly, we have never grounded any of our kids. I am not against extended grounding. We just never used it. By the time they were teenagers, they were pretty dang amazing kids.

We Suggest Finding Their Weakness
We encourage you to try to find what means the most to them. What is their kryptonite? What will bring change to their lives? That is the pain mechanism.

Isolation
In F-5, write in isolation. Isolation can be a very powerful tool, if used correctly (though it can be a very negative tool if used incorrectly). It brings pain for Laken to have to stop playing games for a while. If the kids are not playing well together, it brings pain for them to sit on their beds for 15 minutes. (We don't play on our beds; we sit there and think about what we could do differently). If the pain brings change, that's great. If not, we need to go to the next level.

If you find yourself using isolation for behavior that requires spanking, and you never get to the spanking process, then there is never enough pain to change direction. If so, isolation actually becomes a tool against you.

Most kids do not think about what they did wrong. It's just natural. They think about how stupid isolation is, and how mean you are, and how they hate life.

Before a spanking, my dad would send me to my room. This is a form of isolation. As a kid, I was not sitting there thinking how sorry I was. I was too angry and upset. I got caught. I thought about running away. What happens after the spanking? There is a release. I will get to more of this in just a moment.

I find isolation to be the best for young children. If Peyton starts to cry over something (a whiney little cry because he did not get his way—a scream gets a spanking) I say, "Go sit on your bed until you are done."

One very important point: he does not get to escalate his fit, start to scream loud, or throw a tantrum down the hall. That moves me right into spanking. Peyton goes to his room, then, in a few minutes he comes out and says, "All done, Dad."

"Okay son, we don't cry when we don't get our way."

Most of the time he doesn't even make it to his room before saying, "All done." We are teaching him to control his emotions. This worked for each one of our kids. It now works for my two-year-old granddaughter.

Do this now, and when we are at the store, he has built up that emotion muscle. When I whisper sternly in his ear, "Stop that crying right now," he stops. He realizes that the consequence at the store will not be, "Go to your room." The consequence will involve pain.

If the child is whining, you set the kitchen timer for five minutes and send the kid to his room. That is a form of isolation.

Spanking
In F6, write in spanking. In the next chapter we will go over a lot of the questions parents have about spanking. Does spanking teach children to hit? No. Go to the nursery. The kids that hit and bite are the ones who don't get a spanking. My kids never had that problem.

Does spanking make kids violent? If done improperly and in an abusive fashion, then it obviously will. If done in love, of course not. Once again, go to the schools. Kids that lack discipline are the violent kids; my kids are a pleasure to be around.

Understand that spanking done right will change the heart. Done wrong, spanking will scar the soul. It is very important that you follow the Biblical principles that are discussed.

Please remember, spanking is last resort. You feel like you have exhausted all other avenues, and nothing has changed.

Spanking Principle
We start with a little swat on the bootie of our three-year-old (just barely enough to bring a little pain), or a swat of the hand (once again not abusive, just enough to bring pain). We continue with spankings when appropriate. In the younger years, there are quite a few, but by the age of three, there are barely any. You train the child young.

Some Making Up to Do
For some of you, your kids are older. You have to make up for lost time. Your eight-year-old may get quite a few spankings in the next couple of months. Like any habit, habits are hard to break. The habit of not listening, the habit of not doing what they are told, and the habit of mouthing off must be established. Those habits are hard to break. Be patient and stay your course. Because when pain is greater than reward, the behavior will always change.

Listen Closely to This
Those that spank incorrectly will find themselves spanking for most of the kid's years. Those that spank correctly have most of the spankings out of the way by the time the child is four years old.

The Spanking
This is my experience, and the experience I provide for my children. This is what you need to create in your home. (I will talk

in later chapters about this, but this is for kids that are three years and older).

Mom or Dad would send me to my room. Since we had a consistent standard in the home, I knew what to expect. I didn't sit there guessing what was coming. As I said earlier, I sat there mad—mad at Mom, mad at Dad, mad at the stupid house, and stupid bed, and the stupid dog that kept licking my hand.

Then, Dad would enter. Anger gone, replaced by fear. He quietly sat beside me, looked me in the eye and calmly said, "Why am I in here?" I responded with what I did wrong. He then asked what I should have done. I responded again (by now, with tears in my eyes). He then told me he hated to do this, but he loved me enough to do it.

He then asked me to stand up. I, of course, did. He then grabbed me by the arms near the shoulders, brought me face-to-face (not abusively, but sternly, where I could feel the power of his hands). I could see the tears run down his cheeks. He never yelled, but in a stern, scary whisper of a voice, he said, "You will never do that again."

He squeezed a little harder on my arms so I knew he was serious. He then repeated those words. "You will never do that again." He then put me over his knee, and with his hand, gave me a spanking. Five to eight swats—whatever it took to make me break. He didn't hit me abusively—just enough to make it hurt really bad. He then took me off his knee, held me by the arms and pulled me again up to his tear-drenched face, and repeated, "You will never do that again."

He put me down on the bed and left the room. I, of course, buried my head into my pillow, tears coming down my face. And then in no more than a minute, Dad was sitting beside me. He got me to sit up, wrapped me in his loving arms, and held me tight. He told me he loved me so much, how it was all forgotten and all in the past. And at that moment, something seemed to lift off of me. The rebellious heaviness, that guilt, that junk that comes from doing what you know is wrong, was gone. I was full of peace, joy, and forgiveness. It is amazing that some of the happiest moments of my life came after a spanking. I came out and apologized to Mom, or whomever. And then it was not mentioned again.

Now, Let's Break It Down
First, you are not yelling or screaming. You are not caught up in the emotion. Spanking is done in love. You walk in, sit down, and discuss the wrong behavior. You explain what they should do differently. You are filling the moral warehouse.

At this time, you may get some information you did not know, and this information may change the consequence. If you are calm, you can make sure they receive the right consequence. (They may appeal and have a reason you did not know beforehand).

You ask your child to stand up. (In the next chapter we will discuss what to do if the child doesn't do what you ask or throws a tantrum. If you follow that advice, they will start doing what you ask). You grab the child by the arm, bring them in close and let them know the future. The future is, "You won't do this again!"

You do not shake them. Shaking can cause damage.

You put them over your knee. Men, I strongly recommend the hand. Most importantly I can regulate the pain. Using a belt, I have no idea how much pain is being inflicted. Also, the hand is more personable. (Skeptics might say the hand is for love. Yes, and discipline is love.) My mom spanked with a spoon, and it just was never the same. You lose something when you use an object.

An aside—ladies may have to use a spoon. Because if you are like my mom at all, when Momma did use the hand, it was a gift. Jason and I would scream like we were in pain, and then when she left, we would laugh. We used to always tell her, "Mom, please let Dad spank us, we don't want your spanking."

"She would say, "NO! You are getting a spanking from me!" My heart would jump for joy. By the time your kids get to be five and older, Dad should be doing most, if not all, of the spankings. "Wait until Dad gets home," is a phrase you should use.

Single moms? Don't worry, a spoon will do just fine.

Back to the Spanking
Spank the child with enough force to bring pain. Obviously, you adjust for the age and sex of the child. I would spank my eight-year-old harder than my four-year-old. Boys spank normally harder than girls. And each child will be different. Peyton needed just a couple swats on the backside, while Baylor needed five good ones. Heath's attitude said, "Bring it, Dad. Is that all you got?" Laken cried long before the second swat got to his back side.

Remember, spanking is love. We want to bring just enough pain to overshadow the reward of the bad behavior—just enough pain to break them. You will know when it happens. Sometimes it is three swats (with Heath it was six).

Then, pick the child off your lap, put them down, and leave the room. How long you stay out is determined by the individual child. You should never be out more than a minute.

When Peyton was three, I would simply walk out and then walk right back in. Laken would hyperventilate if I didn't make up with him right away.

Hug the child and say how much you love them. At that moment, the offense is gone. It is in the past. I then add my own personal touch to pull them out of any feelings of guilt. I hug them and then slowly reach down and do a little tickle.

"Baylor, Dad is going to just put his hand under your arm. Don't laugh." Baylor will try hard not to laugh, but then he does, and the mood breaks. He hugs me strongly; he is a happy boy.

Remember, after the spanking, you can't throw their errors in their faces; the forgiveness has come. We hug, we love, and now we go on with life.

Make sure you spank when the flow chart calls for it. Do not let your children's tears keep you from discipline. If you do, you will raise a fool. Do not let the fear of your kids not loving you keep you from discipline. If you do, they will grow up and resent you.

Age-Appropriate Discipline
(The ages listed below are in approximate. As always, children vary.)

Three months – Year and Half:
A gentle but firm voice saying, "No!"

While feeding, the child is not allowed to put hands in food or grab a spoon. If saying no does not work, then gently hold the hands while you feed them. You are starting the process of obedience. When the child becomes mobile, if they are touching something, an outlet, or something bad, we would simply remove them from the outlet and say "no, no." If they keep on with the behavior, we take them to other room. You are slowly introducing them to the idea that the parent is in charge. By the time they are three, there are no surprises for the kids.

Year and Half – Two Years:
A light squeeze of the hand with a "no, no." Once again, you remove them from the temptation. If that doesn't work, then give them a swat on the leg right next to the butt, hard enough to bring a cry. (Remember, the pain has to be enough to change direction.)

For a fit—crying because they did not get their way—they go to their bed or room until they are done. If they escalate (throw themselves on the floor, wail about), they get a firm, "We don't throw a fit!" while I take them to their bed. When they are done, I let them out. You can stand right outside the door and say, "You can get out when you are done. Do you want daddy to close the door?"

Two Years – Four years:
Swat on the leg right around from the butt. You can get a little butt in there. Not enough to leave a welt, just enough to bring a little pain and change. If it doesn't bring a cry, and they do it again, put a little more pain into it. You need enough pain to change direction. This is done, of course, only for foolishness. It has to be really foolish.

With my granddaughter, who I would never spank, I just pick something she hates. She hates fish. I say, "If you don't stop, grandpa will go get a fish." She stops right away. At this age, a little bump on the butt, light, little pain, or do what I do—find something to get them to stop. Remember, discipline is simply changing their direction. If I can do that without a spank, I will do that. Spanking is my last resort.

For a fit, the child still goes to the room. Tantrums and escalated fits are totally unacceptable at this age. You can cry, but you better not throw a fit. Crying is an emotion—we can deal with that. A tantrum is rebellion and has no place in my home. You can be mad, but don't be loud and don't escalate. My kids can cry, but don't let me hear you. Make it quiet. When my daughter Savvy got loud, I got louder. "HEY, WE DON'T THROW A FIT IN MY HOUSE. Get in your room until you're done." This is all it would take.

You will find that fits outside the house will be rare. In a store, they should already know that fits are inappropriate. If you have been dealing with it at home, shopping be fit free.

Every child tries *one* though. Since we do not discipline in public, I usually do the patented little pinch. I will whisper in stern voice, "If you don't stop right now, you will get it." They keep on misbehaving, and I sneakily reach down and give a light pinch on the leg—just enough to bring pain. (Once again, abuse leaves a mark. You want just a little pinch.) The child may give out a scream. We leave the store, and when the child has calmed down, we go back in the store. The next time, I say, "If you don't stop," amazingly, they stop

Four years and older:
Usually what we did above is just fine. A stern word usually solves the problem. Removal solves the problem. But as a last resort, sometimes they need a spanking.

Rules of Spanking
1.   Done only for foolish behavior, and only when the flow chart advises.
2.   Done in love and for the purpose of bringing change. The pain you bring is age appropriate. You spank a four-year-old pretty light, compared to a ten-year-old.
3.   Never abusive! We apply pain, never injury! Abuse is any act of error or authority that endangers or impairs a child's physical or emotional health and development. That is not Biblical spanking! We never spank when we are angry. We calm down and do it right. When you are angry it can turn abusive.
4.   Never done publicly. (My two-year-old may get a slap on the leg in front of family or friends, but never in public. Parents have lost their children for this.) Once the child is four, it should almost always be done in the manner listed, and it should always be done privately. When done in public at the age of four or older, it brings shame and embarrassment. This does not fit within the stated goal of love.
5.   Never a bare bottom. Once again this is shameful and embarrassing. It lacks love.
6.   You never slap a child! This once again is abuse, shameful and not love.

7. You never let the child sit for more than a minute afterward.
8. You restore the relationship afterward, and do not bring it up again.

This Week at Home

Questions for Review

1. What is the purpose of pain? Is pain good or bad?

2. What do you do if your child starts crying because they don't get their way? What do you do if they escalate into a fit?

3. Write out the rules of spanking:

Your Scenario for Discussion:

Your teenager is cutting themselves on purpose. (This behavior is literally called *cutting*.)

CHAPTER 13:
Environment and Spanking Questions

Most of this segment is contained in *More than a Dad*, but just in case you did not read it, we felt it was very important to put it in this chapter.

Anything raised in the wrong environment will not flourish, even when you follow all the right principles. You could have the best seed, the best manure, the best soil, but if it is 10 degrees below zero, the crop will not grow. You have to have right principles and the right environment.

You could follow all the 13 chapters to a tee and do each of them perfectly, but if the home environment is wrong, the child will not grow up with Godly character. Your crops will fail.

Parents it is your job to create a great environment for your children. Here are the keys.

Our Home is a Happy Home
The Joy of the Lord is our strength; we rejoice in the Lord always; again I say rejoice. *Nobody* gets to wake up moody. If your child is moody, too bad. I love you and your future spouse too much to allow you to be grumpy. Go to your room, and you have five minutes to come out happy, or we have to add some correction to your life.

"Well, she is just not a morning person." The Biblical standard—she needs to be. The Bible does not say "rejoice, except in the morning." ALWAYS.

When Dad gets home from work, he doesn't get to be grumpy. If you act like you're happy all the time, at the end of your life, you have lived one happy life.

Parents should make the home a fun and happy place to be. If you do this, your teenagers will not be trying to escape it. They will want to be a part of it. Parents, all married couples fight. Try to keep it to a minimum and keep screaming and meanness to a minimum. Remember, your kids are watching and learning. If you look closely, you can see yourself in your children while they are fighting with each other. If the kids see the fight, make sure they see you make up.

Our Home is a Loving Home
You do not let the kids fight. You do not allow the kids to be mad at each other and especially not at you. The sun never goes down on anyone's anger. Before anyone goes to bed, all is resolved. Your children are told that they are best friends. Kids are taught to see the good in the home, the good in their mom and dad. Parents remind them to focus on the good in life.

Life is about Memories
Set a daily goal to make some great memories with your kids. Schedule a family night each week—same night of the week. (If you don't schedule it, it won't happen.) Those two hours a week (100 hours a year, 1800 hours with your kids living at home) can never be replaced. Those hours will be some of the best hours of your and your children's lives. Don't be like most parents who regret not spending time with the kids.

Make sure each holiday is special. It isn't so much about the gifts, but about the relationships. Make the time to ensure that the holidays are amazing.

Start a Family Activity

This gives your family something to do. It could be hiking, biking, or playing basketball. Whatever it is, it is your family's activity. Buy the bikes, build the hoops and backboards. It's interesting that when you invest in something, it makes you put it to use.

Take Family Vacations
Family vacations are not an option. They are a requirement. They are time away from the house and job responsibilities to just work on your relationships. This has to happen every year. If you don't, you will blink, the kids will be out of the house, and you will have missed 20 epic times with your child.

Some of us have work, but make sure that most of the day is work free. From the time the kids get up in the morning till we go to bed, we are doing family stuff. I usually have a few hours before they get up to take care of my other duties.

Me and Kid Time
When you have more than one child, it is important that you take each child out for just some one-on-one time. It doesn't have to be long (it can be 30 minutes). You need time for just the two of you to build the relationship. You can talk, maybe go get some ice cream.

Moms, it is important to take out your sons. They are learning how to relate to girls, learning how to talk, how to communicate, and how to date. The same goes for daughters and Dad. Five out of seven nights, I make sure I spend some time with each child. It might be playing a game of catch, a video game together, or watching our show. I say, "our show," because Holly and I have shows specific to each child.

Family Identity
Family identity is *who you are as a family unit*. It teaches the kids that we are a team. We work together, we do life together. This is how the Andersons do things. This is the code we live our lives by—the core values of your family.

As parents, get into the habit of using your last name to describe what you do. For example, I often say "Andersons don't quit. Andersons don't give up."

When one of my boys is working on something and gets frustrated and starts to walk away, I say "In five minutes, be back here. Andersons always finish what we start." By doing so, I tell the kids they are part of something bigger than any individual. "You are part of a team, and here is how the team does life."

I say, "Andersons are not grumpy in the morning. Andersons get good grades. Anderson's clean up their table at restaurants. Anderson are on time. Andersons work hard." I hope you get the point. People look for groups to join and teams to celebrate. We want to belong to something.

At my high school, we enjoyed Gilbert Tiger "Pride." It was something special to be a Gilbert Tiger. In the same way, it should be something special to be part of your family. "Andersons love each other. Andersons are best friends. Andersons go to church every week. Anderson's stand for the national anthem. Andersons treat everyone equally. Andersons honor our police.

Andersons are super good looking (we might be too good looking—it's a burden for us Anderson's to so resemble the Greek Gods).

Get into the habit of turning your family into a team.

Double Portion
Your kids always get a more of your great characteristics and more of your compromises. You can either set your kids up or hold them back. Remember, they will do what they see you do, not what they hear you say.

This is why you see generational traits in people's lives. Dad was an alcoholic, and now the kids are. Mom dealt with stress, now the kids deal with stress. A parent had a gambling addiction, now the kids do.

My grandparents had a mess of bad habits from gambling and alcohol abuse to physical abuse. My parents broke that off, and me and my brother didn't have to deal with those problems.

(By the way—when I mention some of these things, I know they are socially acceptable, and to be honest, I don't care if you do them or not. I'm telling you what the Andersons do. The Anderson parents don't have alcohol in their fridge, nor would we ever drink in front of our kids. I don't care if you do but know this the statistics are clear on this. Your kids will have a 300 times higher likelihood of dealing with drug and alcohol problems in their teenager years. It is just a fact. The same goes for Marijuana.)

The Andersons go to church every week. Once again, every statistic shows that kids that attend church every week are happier and more successful.

Look at your parents, at yourself and the things that hold you back. Overcome those things so the kids don't have to

I am your moral Conscience
I said this before, but in our culture, it's important, so I say it again. I make my kid's decisions for them until they can make good decisions. If my child came to me at eight and said they thought they were a horse, I would not get them on medication to make them a horse. We don't allow huge changes that alter the rest of their lives based on feelings.

A girl with anorexia believes she is fat. We don't say "Well, that is her truth." If my thirteen-year-old believed they were something other than how God created them, then my job is to steer them back to the way they were created.

I raise my kids to the Biblical standard. I don't change the Bible to fit the kid. I also would never allow a teacher or anyone to teach my kids about sex, or their beliefs on sex.

Sure, the six-grade class where they separate the boys and girls is fine as long as what they are teaching lines up with our beliefs. Kids are very suspectable at young age. You tell a bunch of third graders, "Do you feel out of place? Do you feel like you don't really belong? Do you sometimes have doubts?" (Surprise! I just described every child on the planet.) Follow up with "That might be because you are confused with your gender" and you're giving them the wrong solution. These days, it's very important that we guard our kid's future. Remember, we raise our kids to the Biblical standard. We don't change the standard for our kids.

Spanking Questions:

Does spanking teach a child to hit, and does it make them violent? Go to any nursery in America. The kids that hit, bite, and are mean are the ones who do not have Biblical discipline in their lives. The kids walking in love, like my children, benefit from Biblical discipline.

Let's be honest. Kids are smarter than a rat. A four-year-old knows the difference between Mom and Dad spanking their backside because they did something wrong and hitting some kid to get their own way. Children that hit others do it because there is no consequence in their lives for their actions. The reward is greater than the consequence.

Remember that anything used incorrectly will bring abuse. A bat used correctly will bring fun to family playing baseball. Used incorrectly, can damage property or people. Does this mean we outlaw the bat? No, the bat is not bad; it is the person using it. Spanking is not bad, unless it is used incorrectly, and then it is abuse. Used correctly it will shape and mold your child's heart.

I go to give my child a spanking and he runs. What do I do?
Since we started with our children at a young age, I have never had this problem, nor did my dad. I never ran because I knew the consequences would greatly outweigh the reward of running. If my son did run, I would calmly explain what the future holds. One, I'm going to catch you, and you are getting a spanking for running. Then after that spanking is over, we will start the spanking process all over. I will come in, you will come to me, and we will perform the original spanking. If they run again, rinse and repeat.

For a four-year-old, I give them a swat telling them never to run from me. Then we give the original spanking. Remember, the consequence for running has to be greater than the reward of defying you.

When I send my child to his room for a spanking, he goes into a tantrum – screaming and pulling things off the wall. What do I do? This advice goes also for screaming while they go to their room. Once again, I understand emotions. You can cry on the way into the room; you can cry in the room. Emotions are fine. I have a problem when it turns into rebellion. It became rebellion when the child screams or throws a fit.

By the age of two, each of my kids had tried this. Once again, the consequence made the reward of rebellion unattractive. Right when rebellion, started I gave a quick warning "You better not throw a fit with me. You will go quietly to your room!" If they continued, I would simply go into the room, or grab them in the hallway and take them into the room. Very sternly, I'd say "Never throw a fit with me." I would then give a light swat to them for the fit. Leave the room. If the fit carried on, I would peek in the room, and let them know if the fit did not stop right now, they would get another spanking for the fit. Amazingly, the fit stopped.

I never had that happen more than two times with each child. (This also goes for a fit after a spanking. You can cry because it hurts, but you do not scream, and you do not throw a fit. Emotions are fine, rebellion emotional blackmail is not.)

My child doesn't cry during a spanking. What should I do? I think the important thing to look for is: did the behavior change? If so, then the spankings are fine. If not, then you are not bringing enough pain to the situation.

My child seems to do fine at home, but in public, he blackmails me with his fits. What should we do? Public fits are tricky. The child knows he has you. Once again, you have to make sure the pain for bad behavior is greater than the reward. You obviously never give into fits—give into just one, and you will have a huge problem on your hands. I have had to leave a store just once with each child, but never again. Many times, I had to whisper in his ear to knock it off and put my little pincher by their bottom. The threat of the pinch was enough.

We are a blended family. Can I spank my stepson? This is a tricky question because it depends on many factors. It depends on the relationship the child has with his parents, depends on the courts, and depends on the child. If I were in a blended family, I wouldn't spank my wife's kids. I felt it would be crossing a line with the other dad. A lot of the time, Mom will have to do it, or you will have to find another source of pain that is greater than the reward (taking away certain privileges). The same answer goes for adopted and foster parents. The law says you cannot, so you don't spank but you have to become creative to change the behavior.

Me and my child got into a power struggle, one spanking after another; what should we do? This has happened to many families, including my parents with Jason when he was three. Jason wanted a drink, they'd said, "Say please." He said, "No." Spanking. Then they said, "Say please." He said, "No." Spanking. Finally, Jason said, "I don't want a drink."

I have never had this happen. I believe that's because I don't set myself up for it. For example, Baylor wants a drink, and I say, "Oops, we forgot something," When the timer goes off, come back and ask correctly. I gave foothold for the struggle to happen. If he doesn't come back, fine, no drink.

I tell my two-year-old not to touch. He touches. I remove him from the temptation. Many parents spank, and then, to test their parenting, they leave the child right next to the object. Human nature hates to be controlled and challenged like that, so the child touches again. Parents spank again. See how you put yourself into that struggle?

Or a parent will say, "Do this." Kid says, "No." Take the kid to the room, spank, and say, "Don't come out until you are ready to do what I ask." No struggle, the child is in a constant state of consequence until he decides to do what I ask. I think most, if not all, power struggles happen because we provide the environment for them to take place.

Back to the don't touch example. What is interesting is that if you act like you are not watching them, they will not touch it again.

Scriptures for Spanking

> Proverbs 26:3
> *"A whip for the horse, a bridle for the donkey, and a rod for the back of fools."*
>
> Proverbs 23:13-14
> *"Do not hold back discipline from the child. Although you beat him with the rod, he will not die. You shall beat him with the rod and deliver his soul from foolishness."*
>
> Proverbs 22:15
> *"Foolishness is bound up in the heart of a child, but the rod of discipline will remove it far from him."*

Proverbs 29:15 (NASB)
"The rod and reproof give wisdom, but a child who gets his own way brings shame to his mother."

Proverbs 10:13 (NASB)
"On the lips of the discerning, wisdom is found, but a rod is for the back of him who lacks understanding."

Proverbs 19:18 (NKJV)
"Chasten your son while there is hope, and do not set your heart on his destruction."

Proverbs 13:24 (God's Word edition)
"Whoever refuses to spank his son hates him, but whoever loves his son disciplines him from early on."

Proverbs 23:13-14 (God's Word edition)
"Do not hesitate to discipline a child. If you spank him, he will not die. Spank him yourself, and you will save his soul from hell."

Dear Parent(s),

Congratulations! We hope you enjoyed this program. We hope God was able to use us and use this book to help instill Biblical truths into you so you can go forth in confidence and train up your children in the way they should go.

Guess what? They will not depart from the path you lay out. They will bring joy and happiness to you for all of your days. The character you put in them will change generations to come.

Go back through all the scenarios and see how you would handle them now that you've finished the class. We highly encourage you to do what we did—go through the class every year. You seem to hear only what applies to the season you are in. You'll find that you'll go through class again and say, "Oh, we got a teenager now, we need to do this, and do that." You'll also remind yourself of the little things you got away from—things that make such a huge difference.

Thank you for all your time and your support; may God lead you, guide you, and bless all that you do. Please look us up on social media. Our teachings can always be seen at www.livingwordonline.com.

Your friends,

Scot and Holly Anderson

Would you like to have Scot speak at your conference, church, school…?

Scot will carefully customize his talk for you and your audience.

Contact us today for full information on booking Scot to speak at your next meeting or conference.

Visit:
www.scotandersonministries.com
or call 480-964-4463.

Printed in Great Britain
by Amazon

59839527R00157